# NAVAL POSTGRADUATE SCHOOL

MONTEREY, CALIFORNIA

# THESIS

---

**FEMALE GENITAL MUTILATION: A DIFFERENT KIND OF TERRORISM**

by

Kristie L. Krebs

June 2019

Co-Advisors: Carolyn C. Halladay
Rachel L. Sigman

---

**Approved for public release. Distribution is unlimited.**

This thesis contains images that readers may find disturbing. They are included to support the researcher's primary claim that female genital mutilation is tantamount to terrorism.

THIS PAGE INTENTIONALLY LEFT BLANK

Approved for public release. Distribution is unlimited.

This thesis contains images that readers may find disturbing. They are included to support the researcher's primary claim that female genital mutilation is tantamount to terrorism.

# FEMALE GENITAL MUTILATION: A DIFFERENT KIND OF TERRORISM

Kristie L. Krebs
U.S. Citizenship and Immigration Services, Department of Homeland Security
BA, College of Notre Dame of Maryland, 1998

Submitted in partial fulfillment of the
requirements for the degree of

## MASTER OF ARTS IN SECURITY STUDIES
## (HOMELAND SECURITY AND DEFENSE)

from the

## NAVAL POSTGRADUATE SCHOOL
## June 2019

Approved by:    Carolyn C. Halladay
Co-Advisor

Rachel L. Sigman
Co-Advisor

Erik J. Dahl
Associate Chair for Instruction
Department of National Security Affairs

THIS PAGE INTENTIONALLY LEFT BLANK

# ABSTRACT

This thesis demonstrates that in addition to constituting a human rights violation, female genital mutilation can also function as a form of terrorism against women and girls. Much like a terrorist act, female genital mutilation is carried out to influence the attitudes and behavior of a wider target audience. Specifically, female genital mutilation is a violent act that perpetuates society's control over women and influences gender inequality. A basic assessment of female genital mutilation against the core characteristics of terrorism reveals that, in many instances, all the elements commonly accepted by scholars who define terrorism are found within female genital mutilation. By demonstrating how female genital mutilation can function as a terrorist act, this thesis offers another category for experts to explore in the evolution of the phenomenon known as terrorism: gender-based terrorism.

THIS PAGE INTENTIONALLY LEFT BLANK

# ABSTRACT

This thesis demonstrates that in addition to constituting a human rights violation, female genital mutilation can also function as a form of terrorism against women and girls. Much like a terrorist act, female genital mutilation is carried out to influence the attitudes and behavior of a wider target audience. Specifically, female genital mutilation is a violent act that perpetuates society's control over women and influences gender inequality. A basic assessment of female genital mutilation against the core characteristics of terrorism reveals that, in many instances, all the elements commonly accepted by scholars who define terrorism are found within female genital mutilation. By demonstrating how female genital mutilation can function as a terrorist act, this thesis offers another category for experts to explore in the evolution of the phenomenon known as terrorism: gender-based terrorism.

THIS PAGE INTENTIONALLY LEFT BLANK

# TABLE OF CONTENTS

| | | | |
|---|---|---|---|
| I. | INTRODUCTION | | 1 |
| | A. | RESEARCH QUESTION | 2 |
| | B. | RESEARCH DESIGN | 3 |
| | C. | LITERATURE REVIEW | 4 |
| | | 1. Female Genital Mutilation as a Human Rights Violation | 4 |
| | | 2. Criminalization of Female Genital Mutilation in the United States | 9 |
| | | 3. Understanding Terrorism | 11 |
| | D. | CHAPTER OVERVIEW | 13 |
| II. | FEMALE GENITAL MUTILATION | | 15 |
| | A. | BACKGROUND | 15 |
| | B. | TYPES | 16 |
| | C. | TERMINOLOGY | 20 |
| | D. | TRADITIONAL AND MEDICAL PRACTITIONERS | 21 |
| | E. | IMMEDIATE HEALTH COMPLICATIONS AND LONG-TERM CONSEQUENCES | 24 |
| III. | ANALYSIS | | 29 |
| | A. | DOES FEMALE GENITAL MUTILATION INVOLVE A THREAT OR USE OF FORCE? | 29 |
| | B. | DOES FEMALE GENITAL MUTILATION INVOLVE AN INTENT TO INFLUENCE POLITICAL OR SOCIAL SITUATIONS? | 31 |
| | | 1. Sociocultural Reasons | 32 |
| | | 2. Psychosexual Reasons | 34 |
| | | 3. Socioeconomic Reasons | 36 |
| | | 4. Religious Reasons | 36 |
| | | 5. Hygiene and Aesthetic Reasons | 38 |
| | | 6. Summary of Reasons | 38 |
| | C. | DOES FEMALE GENITAL MUTILATION AFFECT AN AUDIENCE BEYOND THOSE DIRECTLY TARGETED BY TARGETING THOSE TRADITIONALLY PERCEIVED AS NON-COMBATANTS, IN AN EFFORT TO CREATE FEAR? | 39 |
| | D. | SUMMARY OF FINDINGS | 46 |
| IV. | CONCLUSION AND RECOMMENDATIONS | | 47 |

**LIST OF REFERENCES ................................................................................................. 51**

**INITIAL DISTRIBUTION LIST .................................................................................... 59**

# LIST OF FIGURES

| | | |
|---|---|---|
| Figure 1. | Types of female genital mutilation | 17 |
| Figure 2. | Type II female genital mutilation on a one-year-old girl | 18 |
| Figure 3. | Girl with her legs bound together after Type III infibulation | 19 |
| Figure 4. | Type III infibulation with the urethral and vaginal orifices | 19 |
| Figure 5. | Female genital mutilation performed on a young girl by traditional practitioners | 23 |
| Figure 6. | Tools used to perform female genital mutilation | 23 |
| Figure 7. | A Kurdish girl—whose mother tells her she is going to a party—is taken to her neighbor's house where a midwife cuts her genitalia while other girls wait outside to undergo the same | 40 |
| Figure 8. | In Uganda, people gather around girls of the Sebei tribe who have just undergone female genital mutilation | 41 |
| Figure 9. | Pokot girls in Kenya seated on rocks during a ceremony for female genital mutilation | 41 |
| Figure 10. | Female genital mutilation ceremony in Sierra Leone | 42 |
| Figure 11. | Female genital mutilation ceremony in the Gorontalo province of Indonesia | 44 |
| Figure 12. | Kuria girls in Kenya being paraded after undergoing female genital mutilation | 45 |

THIS PAGE INTENTIONALLY LEFT BLANK

# LIST OF TABLES

Table 1. Primary reasons for the practice of female genital mutilation and their link to intent to influence political or social situations......................39

THIS PAGE INTENTIONALLY LEFT BLANK

# LIST OF ACRONYMS AND ABBREVIATIONS

| | |
|---|---|
| CAT | Convention against Torture |
| CEDAW | Convention on the Elimination of All Forms of Discrimination against Women |
| CRC | Convention on the Rights of the Child |
| ICCPR | International Covenant on Civil and Political Rights |
| PRB | Populations Reference Bureau |
| UDHR | Universal Declaration of Human Rights |
| UN | United Nations |
| UNICEF | United Nations International Children's Emergency Fund |
| UNFPA | United Nations Population Fund |
| WHO | World Health Organization |

THIS PAGE INTENTIONALLY LEFT BLANK

# EXECUTIVE SUMMARY

This thesis examines whether female genital mutilation, in addition to constituting a human rights violation, can also be categorized as an act of terrorism. Female genital mutilation is appropriate to explore in this context given that, much like a terrorist act, it is carried out as a form of communication. Female genital mutilation is a violent act that perpetuates society's control over women and communicates gender inequality.[1] Similarly, terrorism is a violent act used to "influence the attitudes and behavior of a wider target audience."[2]

Currently, female genital mutilation is recognized under international law as a human rights violation, as discrimination and violence against women, and as torture, yet practicing societies within certain parts of Africa, the Middle East, and Asia defend the practice as a requirement of their culture.[3] The practice entails "the partial or total removal of the external female genitalia, or other injury to the female genital organs" without medical reason.[4] Girls are often held down while their legs are forced apart and their genitalia are cut with a crude instrument and absent use of anesthesia.[5]

The number of girls affected by female genital mutilation is unthinkable. There are an estimated 200 million women and girls alive today who have had female genital

---

[1] World Health Organization (WHO), *Eliminating Female Genital Mutilation: An Interagency Statement* (Geneva, Switzerland: World Health Organization, 2008), 5, https://www.who.int/reproductivehealth/publications/fgm/9789241596442/en/.

[2] Jeffrey M. Bale and Gary Ackerman, *Recommendations on the Development of Methodologies and Attributes for Assessing Terrorist Threats of WMD Terrorism* (Monterey, CA: Monterey Institute of International Studies), 6, https://courses.cs.washington.edu/courses/csep590/05au/readings/Bale_Ackerman_FinalReport.pdf.

[3] "What International Human Rights Law Says about Female Genital Mutilation," Equality Now, accessed February 7, 2019, https://d3n8a8pro7vhmx.cloudfront.net/equalitynow/pages/265/attachments/original/1527182447/FGM_Under_International_Law_EN.pdf?1527182447; "Female Genital Mutilation," WHO, January 31, 2018, https://www.who.int/news-room/fact-sheets/detail/female-genital-mutilation.

[4] WHO, "Female Genital Mutilation."

[5] Patricia A. Broussard, "Female Genital Mutilation: Exploring Strategies for Ending Ritualized Torture; Shaming, Blaming, and Utilizing the Convention against Torture," *Duke Journal of Gender Law and Policy* 15, no. 19 (2008): 24, https://scholarship.law.duke.edu/djglp/vol15/iss2/2.

mutilation performed on them.[6] Approximately 3 million women and girls across the globe are at risk of the procedure each year, including women and girls in the United States.[7] Despite these massive numbers, and despite the fact that female genital mutilation influences gender inequality throughout the societies where it is practiced, it has not been examined as a form of terrorism.[8]

To determine if there is a nexus between female genital mutilation and terrorism, this thesis provides an understanding of female genital mutilation and then analyzes the practice against the core elements of terrorism: 1) "the threat or use of force" 2) "with the intent to influence political or social situations" 3) "by affecting an audience beyond those directly targeted," and "targeting those traditionally perceived as non-combatants in an effort to create fear."[9]

The analysis chapter of this thesis demonstrates that in many instances, all the elements commonly accepted by scholars who define terrorism are found within the practice of female genital mutilation. Ultimately, the practice serves as a violent means to control the female segment of a population and maintain gender inequality. The practice affects an audience beyond the girl or woman being cut and, in many cases, the violence is exposed through ceremonies and rituals. While the threat and use of violence does not manifest as a gun or a bomb, the very personal invasion of the body through which it does manifest, including the dishonor and social sanctions that come from not complying, is just as real and devastating.

Although the hands that perform and facilitate female genital mutilation seem very different from the hands that have committed terrorist acts under names such as ISIS, Hezbollah, or the Ku Klux Klan, this thesis concludes that female genital mutilation can

---

[6] "Sexual and Reproductive Health: Female Genital Mutilation (FGM)," WHO, accessed May 23, 2018, http://www.who.int/reproductivehealth/topics/fgm/prevalence/en.

[7] WHO.

[8] WHO, *Eliminating Female Genital Mutilation*, 5.

[9] David Brannan, Kristin Darken, and Anders Strindberg, *A Practitioner's Way Forward: Terrorism Analysis* (Salinas, CA: Agile Press, 2014), 43.

be used as a terrorist act against women and girls. Specifically, the practice can serve as a form of gender-based terrorism, and yet gender-based terrorism is not indicated across the current typologies of terrorism. Therefore, by demonstrating how female genital mutilation can function as terrorism, this thesis offers gender-based terrorism as another category for experts to explore in the evolution of the phenomenon known as terrorism.

THIS PAGE INTENTIONALLY LEFT BLANK

# I. INTRODUCTION

> Terrorism is specifically designed to have far-reaching psychological effects beyond the immediate victim(s) or object of the terrorist attack. It is meant to instill fear within, and thereby intimidate, a wider target audience that might include a rival ethnic or religious group, an entire country, a national government or political party, or public opinion in general.
>
> —Bruce Hoffman, *Inside Terrorism*[1]

There are an estimated 200 million women and girls alive today who have had female genital mutilation performed on them.[2] This procedure entails "the partial or total removal of the external female genitalia, or other injury to the female genital organs" without medical reason.[3] Girls are often held down while their legs are forced apart and their genitalia are cut with a crude instrument, absent of anesthesia.[4] The procedure is recognized under international law as a human rights violation, as discrimination and violence against women, and as torture, yet practicing societies within certain parts of Africa, the Middle East, and Asia defend it as a requirement of their culture.[5] According to the World Health Organization (WHO), "in every society in which it is practiced, female genital mutilation is a manifestation of gender inequality that is deeply entrenched in the

---

[1] Bruce Hoffman, *Inside Terrorism* (New York: Columbia University Press, 2006), 40.

[2] "Sexual and Reproductive Health: Female Genital Mutilation (FGM)," World Health Organization (WHO), accessed May 23, 2018, http://www.who.int/reproductivehealth/topics/fgm/prevalence/en.

[3] "Female Genital Mutilation," World Health Organization, January 31, 2018, http://www.who.int/news-room/fact-sheets/detail/female-genital-mutilation.

[4] Patricia A. Broussard, "Female Genital Mutilation: Exploring Strategies for Ending Ritualized Torture; Shaming, Blaming, and Utilizing the Convention against Torture," *Duke Journal of Gender Law and Policy* 15, no. 19 (2008): 24, https://scholarship.law.duke.edu/djglp/vol15/iss2/2.

[5] "What International Human Rights Law Says about Female Genital Mutilation," Equality Now, accessed February 7, 2019, https://d3n8a8pro7vhmx.cloudfront.net/equalitynow/pages/265/attachments/original/1527182447/FGM_Under_International_Law_EN.pdf?1527182447; WHO, "Female Genital Mutilation."

social, economic and political structures."[6] Where the practice is prevalent, it "represents society's control over women."[7]

The number of women and girls at risk of female genital mutilation is unthinkable. Every year, approximately three million women and girls across the globe are at risk of the procedure, including women and girls in the United States.[8] A report issued in 2013 by the Population Reference Bureau (PRB) indicates that around 507,000 women and girls in the United States have undergone female genital mutilation or are at risk of having it performed on them.[9] This figure had already more than doubled since PRB's analysis in 2000, which reflected an estimated 228,000 women and girls at risk.[10] This increase is primarily attributed to a rise in immigration of people to the United States from countries where the practice is concentrated.[11]

Despite the massive number of women and girls that female genital mutilation affects, and that the practice influences gender inequality throughout the societies where it is carried out, it has not been examined as a form of terrorism.[12]

## A. RESEARCH QUESTION

This thesis asks the question: In addition to constituting a human rights violation, can female genital mutilation also be categorized as an act of terrorism? With the understanding that there are various motives for performing female genital mutilation, this

---

[6] World Health Organization, *Eliminating Female Genital Mutilation: An Interagency Statement* (Geneva, Switzerland: World Health Organization, 2008), 5, https://www.who.int/reproductivehealth/publications/fgm/9789241596442/en/.

[7] WHO, 5.

[8] WHO, "Sexual and Reproductive Health."

[9] "Women and Girls at Risk of Female Genital Mutilation/Cutting in the United States," Population Reference Bureau, February 5, 2016, https://www.prb.org/us-fgmc/.

[10] Population Reference Bureau.

[11] Population Reference Bureau.

[12] WHO, *Eliminating Female Genital Mutilation*, 5.

thesis also seeks to determine the circumstances that must exist for the practice to meet the criteria to be considered an act of terrorism.

Female genital mutilation is appropriate to explore in this context given that, much like a terrorist act, it is carried out as a form of communication. A distinguishing characteristic of a terrorist act that makes it more than just an act of violence is the message that it generates.[13] Terrorism is used to "influence the attitudes and behavior of a wider target audience" while the victims of terrorist attacks are "viewed as symbolizing something larger or representing a broader category of persons."[14] Female genital mutilation is an act that perpetuates society's control over women, which influences gender inequality.[15] In this respect, the practice may be more than solely a human rights violation.

## B. RESEARCH DESIGN

To determine if there is a nexus between female genital mutilation and terrorism, this thesis analyzes the procedure against the core elements of terrorism: 1) "the threat or use of force" 2) "with the intent to influence political or social situations" 3) "by affecting an audience beyond those directly targeted," and "targeting those traditionally perceived as non-combatants in an effort to create fear."[16]

The scope of this thesis does not include an examination of how and why female genital mutilation is performed within each practicing society. There are various degrees of female genital mutilation and the type performed is determined by the ethnicity or national origin of those practicing it.[17] The World Health Organization (WHO) classifies

---

[13] Jeffrey M. Bale and Gary Ackerman, *Recommendations on the Development of Methodologies and Attributes for Assessing Terrorist Threats of WMD Terrorism* (Monterey, CA: Monterey Institute of International Studies), 6. https://courses.cs.washington.edu/courses/csep590/05au/readings/Bale_Ackerman_FinalReport.pdf.

[14] Bale and Ackerman, 6.

[15] WHO, *Eliminating Female Genital Mutilation*, 5.

[16] David Brannan, Kristin Darken, and Anders Strindberg, *A Practitioner's Way Forward: Terrorism Analysis* (Salinas, CA: Agile Press, 2014), 43.

[17] WHO, *Eliminating Female Genital Mutilation*, 10; World Health Organization, "Sexual and Reproductive Health."

female genital mutilation into four types: 1) clitoridectomy, 2) excision, 3) infibulation, and 4) all other harmful procedures to the female genitalia for non-medical purposes.[18] WHO explains that there has been inadequate research conducted on the fourth classification; therefore, this thesis is limited to discussion surrounding clitoridectomy, excision, and infibulation.[19]

The reasons for the procedure also vary across practicing societies.[20] To narrow the scope of research, the focus of this thesis is limited to the five primary reasons cited across literature for continuing the practice of female genital mutilation: sociocultural, psychosexual, socioeconomic, religious, and hygiene and aesthetics.[21] With limited information on female genital mutilation in the United States, this thesis draws on various studies from around the world where the practice is prevalent.

### C. LITERATURE REVIEW

As there is currently no literature that explores female genital mutilation through the lens of terrorism, the first part of this review focuses on how the practice evolved to be seen as a human rights violation. The second part provides information on the criminalization of female genital mutilation in the United States. The last part of this review provides an understanding of the phenomenon known as terrorism.

#### 1. Female Genital Mutilation as a Human Rights Violation

Female genital mutilation is presently recognized as a human rights violation through various treaties, along with "General Comments/Recommendations of treaty monitoring bodies, and consensus documents."[22] Long before the procedure was identified

---

[18] WHO, *Eliminating Female Genital Mutilation*, 10.

[19] WHO, "Sexual and Reproductive Health."

[20] WHO.

[21] "Female Genital Mutilation (FGM) Frequently Asked Questions," United Nations Population Fund, accessed July 9, 2018, https://www.unfpa.org/resources/female-genital-mutilation-fgm-frequently-asked-questions.

[22] Equality Now, "International Human Rights Law."

as a human rights violation, the topic was considered taboo and therefore one that governments chose to avoid.[23] For years, the practice was viewed as outside the scope of international human rights law.[24] Violence against women was largely seen "as a private act or a domestic matter carried out by private individuals."[25] It was not until the 1990s, when it was examined against various international instruments within the United Nations (UN), that female genital mutilation was classified as a human rights violation.[26]

When it initially gained attention by international organizations, the focus centered on female genital mutilation as a health concern.[27] In 1979, WHO convened the first international conference that addressed the damaging health consequences of the practice on women and girls.[28] During the conference, WHO, along with the United Nations International Children's Emergency Fund (UNICEF) and the United Nations Population Fund (UNFPA), issued a joint statement proclaiming that female genital mutilation severely endangers women's health and violates their right to the highest attainment of health.[29] Once viewed in this light, the practice then evolved into a human rights issue from the viewpoint of health as a human rights argument.[30]

---

[23] Hamid Rushwan, "Female Genital Mutilation: A Tragedy for Women's Reproductive Health," *African Journal of Urology* 19, no. 3 (September 2013): 130–133, https://doi.org/10.1016/j.afju.2013.03.002.

[24] United Nations Population Fund, *Implementation of the International and Regional Human Rights Framework for the Elimination of Female Genital Mutilation* (New York: United Nations Population Fund), 8, https://www.unfpa.org/sites/default/files/pub-pdf/FGMC-humanrights.pdf.

[25] United Nations Population Fund, 8.

[26] United Nations International Children's Emergency Fund (UNICEF), *Female Genital Mutilation and Cutting: A Statistical Overview and Exploration of the Dynamics of Change* (New York: UNICEF, 2013), 7, http://data.unicef.org/wp-content/uploads/2015/12/FGMC_Lo_res_Final_26.pdf.

[27] UNICEF, 7.

[28] Waleed Sweileh, "Bibliometric Analysis of Literature on Female Genital Mutilation: (1930–2015)," *Reproductive Health* 13, no. 1 (October 2016): 8, https://doi.org/10.1186/s12978-016-0243-8.

[29] Sweileh, 8; Jane Muthumbi et al., "Female Genital Mutilation: A Literature Review of the Current Status of Legislation and Policies in 27 African Countries and Yemen," *African Journal of Reproductive Health* 19, no. 3 (September 2015): 33, https://www.ajol.info/index.php/ajrh/article/view/124907/114424.

[30] Preston Mitchum, "Slapping the Hand of Cultural Relativism: Female Genital Mutilation, Male Dominance, and Health as a Human Rights Framework," *William & Mary Journal of Women and the Law* 19, no. 3 (2013): 599, http://scholarship.law.wm.edu/wmjowl/vol19/iss3/4.

According to an article by Preston Mitchum in the *William and Mary Journal of Women and the Law*, "the earliest recognition of health as a human rights violation was in the constitution of the WHO."[31] The WHO constitution provides that "health is a state of complete physical, mental and social well-being and not merely the absence of disease or infirmity."[32] Mitchum explains that "protecting the right to health is not necessarily only about access to medicines but also involves an overall concern for social, mental, and physical being." In societies where female genital mutilation is practiced, Mitchum says, women are not treated equally as they are not afforded equal opportunities to work, marry, or to maintain their own bodily integrity. Mitchum also explains that "when health is viewed in a wide-ranging context, it becomes clear that it is impossible to protect health without safeguarding basic human rights."[33]

Although there are no specific articles within international human rights instruments that speak directly to female genital mutilation, the Universal Declaration of Human Rights (UDHR) serves as the benchmark to evaluate the practice as a human rights violation.[34] Article 25 of UDHR indicates that "everyone has the right to a standard of living adequate for health and well-being and has been used to argue that FGM/C [female genital mutilation] violates the right to health and bodily integrity."[35] The Vienna World Conference on Human Rights in 1993 is also cited in various publications as a significant event in the classification of female genital mutilation as a human rights violation.[36] During this conference, the practice was designated as "a form of violence against women"

---

[31] Mitchum, 596.

[32] Mitchum, 596.

[33] Mitchum, 598.

[34] UNICEF, *Female Genital Mutilation and Cutting*, 8; Mitchum, "Slapping the Hand of Cultural Relativism," 597.

[35] UNICEF, *Female Genital Mutilation and Cutting*, 8.

[36] Bettina Shell-Duncan, "From Health to Human Rights: Female Genital Cutting and the Politics of Intervention," *American Anthropologist* 110, no. 2 (June 2008): 227, https://doi.org/10.1111/j.1548-1433.2008.00028.x.

while the matter of violence against women "was for the first time acknowledged to fall under the purview of international human rights law."[37]

Once classified as a form of violence against women, the practice could then be examined under the framework of the UN Convention on the Elimination of All Forms of Discrimination against Women (CEDAW).[38] CEDAW is an international human rights treaty adopted by the UN General Assembly in 1979 and is often referred to as the international human rights bill for women.[39] Under CEDAW, female genital mutilation was found to violate the right to be free from gender discrimination as well as the right to physical and mental integrity, including freedom from violence.[40] Article 12 of CEDAW provides that parties "shall take all appropriate measures to eliminate discrimination against women in the field of health care in order to ensure, on the basis of equality of men and women, access to health care services."[41]

CEDAW released a recommendation in 1993 that "categorized gender-based violence as infringing on women's human rights and fundamental freedoms" under general international law.[42] The recommendation also clarified that fundamental freedoms comprise the "right to the highest standard attainable of physical and mental health."[43] Article 5 of CEDAW established an obligation for nations to "modify the social and cultural practices of conduct of men and women, with a view to achieving the elimination

---

[37] Shell-Duncan, 227.

[38] Shell-Duncan, 227.

[39] "Convention on the Elimination of All Forms of Discrimination against Women," United Nations Human Rights Office of the High Commissioner, accessed August 11, 2018, https://www.ohchr.org/en/professionalinterest/pages/cedaw.aspx.

[40] United Nations Population Fund, *International and Regional Human Rights Framework*, 28.

[41] Mitchum, "Slapping the Hand of Cultural Relativism," 598.

[42] Mitchum, 599.

[43] Mitchum, 599; "Convention on the Elimination of All forms of Discrimination against Women," United Nations, accessed September 16, 2018, http://www.un.org/womenwatch/daw/cedaw/recommendations/recomm.htm.

of prejudices and customary and all other practices where are based on the idea of [gender inequality]."[44]

Because female genital mutilation is routinely performed on young girls, the practice also violates the right of the child per the Convention on the Rights of the Child (CRC).[45] As children are largely unable to "protect themselves or make informed decisions about matters that may affect them for the rest of their lives ... international human rights law grants children special protections, codified in the CRC."[46] The CRC also references traditional practices, indicating that "States Parties shall take all effective and appropriate measures with a view to abolishing traditional practices prejudicial to the health of children."[47]

According to UNFPA, female genital mutilation violates "the right not to be subjected to torture or inhuman or degrading treatment or punishment" as related to the protections within the Convention against Torture and Other Cruel, Inhuman, or Degrading Treatment or Punishment.[48] The Committee against Torture (CAT) specifically indicates that the practice is within CAT's mandate.[49] Further, the UN Special Rapporteur on violence against women and the UN Special Rapporteur on torture have both indicated that female genital mutilation "can amount to torture under CAT."[50]

The UDHR and International Covenant on Civil and Political Rights (ICCPR), along with other human rights instruments, also preserve the right for individuals not to be subjected to torture.[51] With regard to children, the CRC provides that "no child shall be

---

[44] Shell-Duncan, "From Health to Human Rights," 227; United Nations, "Convention on the Elimination of All Forms of Discrimination against Women."

[45] United Nations Population Fund, *International and Regional Human Rights Framework*, 32.

[46] United Nations Population Fund, 32.

[47] United Nations Population Fund, 32.

[48] United Nations Population Fund, 30.

[49] United Nations Population Fund, 30.

[50] United Nations Population Fund, 30.

[51] United Nations Population Fund, 31–32.

subjected to torture or other cruel, inhuman or degrading treatment or punishment."[52] Additionally, in extreme instances where female genital mutilation results in death, the practice violates the right to life, which also falls under the UDHR and ICCPR.[53] The UDHR indicates that "everyone has the right to life, liberty and security of person," while the ICCPR states that "every human being has the inherent right to life."[54]

With respect to the long-standing defense of female genital mutilation as a cultural practice, supporters of the practice argue that the government should not stand in the way of people's rights to participate in their culture and religion.[55] UNFPA explained that

> although the international human rights framework has recognized the right to culture, the rights of minorities and the right to religious freedom, these rights are not absolute, and international human rights law recognizes prescribed limitations.... UN treaty monitoring bodies and other human rights mechanisms have clarified that culture and religion cannot be invoked to justify the violation of the rights of women and girls.[56]

Following the UN's classification of female genital mutilation as a human rights violation, many countries, including those where female genital mutilation is prevalent and those that receive large immigrant populations like the United States, have criminalized the practice through legislative measures.[57]

### 2. Criminalization of Female Genital Mutilation in the United States

The U.S. government condemns female genital mutilation, regardless of the reason it is carried out.[58] In 1996, Congress made the practice a federal crime with the passage of

---

[52] United Nations Population Fund, 32.

[53] United Nations Population Fund, 28.

[54] United Nations Population Fund, 28.

[55] United Nations Population Fund, 34.

[56] United Nations Population Fund, 26.

[57] United Nations Population Fund, "Female Genital mutilation (FGM) Frequently Asked Questions."

[58] "U.S. Government Fact Sheet on Female Genital Mutilation or Cutting (FGM/C)," U.S. Department of State, accessed August 11, 2018, https://travel.state.gov/content/travel/en/us-visas/visa-information-resources/fact-sheet-on-female-genital-mutilation-or-cutting.html.

the Federal Prohibition of Female Genital Mutilation Act (18 U.S.C. 116).[59] The act provides that "whoever knowingly circumcises, excises, or infibulates the whole or any part of the labia majora or labia minora or clitoris of another person who has not attained the age of 18 years shall be fined under this title or imprisoned not more than 5 years, or both."[60] The law also provides that "no account shall be taken of the effect on the person on whom the operation is to be performed of any belief on the part of that person, or any other person, that the operation is required as a matter of custom or ritual."[61]

The law was amended in 2013 to address the issue of transporting girls overseas to be cut, known as "vacation cutting."[62] During the early part of summer, after school breaks for summer vacation, parents tell their daughters they are traveling abroad to visit extended family in their parents' country of origin; however, once there, they are forced to undergo female genital mutilation.[63] In an effort to address this issue, Congress amended the 1996 statute by enacting the Transport for Female Genital Mutilation Act in 2013.[64] The 2013 law made it illegal, punishable with up to five years in prison, to knowingly transport girls abroad for the purpose of genital mutilation.[65]

Prior to the enactment of federal legislation, several U.S. states passed legislation against female genital mutilation, starting with Minnesota in 1994.[66] There are presently

---

[59] U.S. Department of State, "18 U.S. Code § 116—Female Genital Mutilation," Legal Information Institute, accessed December 25, 2018, https://www.law.cornell.edu/uscode/text/18/116.

[60] Legal Information Institute, "Female Genital Mutilation."

[61] Legal Information Institute.

[62] "Vacation Cutting: An Illegal Practice Still Running Rampant," AHA Foundation, accessed July 29, 2018, https://www.theahafoundation.org/vacation-cutting-an-illegal-practice-still-running-rampant.

[63] AHA Foundation.

[64] Howard Goldberg et al., "Women and Girls at Risk for Genital Mutilation in the U.S.," *Public Health Reports* 131, no. 2 (March–April 2016): 341, https://doi.org/10.1177/003335491613100218.

[65] AHA Foundation, "Vacation Cutting."

[66] Center for Reproductive Rights, "Legislation on Female Genital Mutilation in the United States" (briefing paper, Center for Reproductive Rights, November 2014), 5–7, www.reproductiverights.org/sites/default/files/documents/pub_bp_fgmlawsusa.pdf.

twenty-eight states with laws against the practice.[67] The statutory language differs across states, criminalizing the practice as a felony offense, yet varies with such specific provisions as vacation cutting.[68] For instance, such states as Texas and Florida include a provision criminalizing vacation cutting, while states like New York and California do not.[69]

Although states that criminalize the practice and the U.S. government view female genital mutilation as a violation of human rights, as child abuse, and as gender-based violence; there is no instance at a federal or state level where female genital mutilation has been considered a form of terrorism against women and girls.[70]

### 3. Understanding Terrorism

A challenging aspect of classifying female genital mutilation as an act of terrorism is the absence of a universally accepted definition of the term *terrorism*. Some publications reference the existence of over 200 definitions of the term.[71] Even throughout the departments and agencies within the U.S. government, the term is described in various ways.

The U.S. Department of Defense defines terrorism as "the unlawful use—or threatened use of—force or violence against individuals or property to coerce or intimidate governments or societies, often to achieve political, religious, or ideological objectives."[72] The U.S. Department of State describes terrorism as "premeditated, politically motivated

---

[67] "FGM Legislation by State," AHA Foundation, accessed July 29, 2018, https://www.theahafoundation.org/female-genital-mutilation/fgm-legislation-by-state/.

[68] AHA Foundation.

[69] AHA Foundation.

[70] U.S. Department of State, "Fact Sheet on Female Genital Mutilation."

[71] Alex Schmid, ed., *The Routledge Handbook of Terrorism Research* (Abingdon, NY: Taylor and Francis, 2011), 39.

[72] Nadav Morag, "Introduction to Terrorism: Typology, Targets and Organization" (lecture, Naval Postgraduate School Center for Homeland Defense and Security, Monterey, CA, April 2015), https://www.chds.us/coursefiles/comp/lectures/NS3028_Intro_to_Terrorism_v02/player.html.

violence perpetrated against noncombatant targets by subnational groups or clandestine agents, usually intended to influence an audience," while the Federal Bureau of Investigation defines terrorism as "the unlawful use of force or violence against persons or property to intimidate or coerce a Government, the civilian population, or any segment thereof, in furtherance of political or social objectives.[73]

### a. *Core Characteristics of Terrorism*

Absent a single definition of terrorism, it is therefore central to the analysis of this thesis to identify the core characteristics of a terrorist act that differentiate it from other forms of violence and compare those elements against female genital mutilation.[74]

Scholars Dr. Alex Schmid and Albert Jongman conducted a content analysis of the various definitions found across academic and government sources to identify the primary elements of terrorism.[75] Schmid and Jongman's study revealed that "the concept of violence emerged in 83.5% of definitions; political goals emerged in 65%; causing fear and terror in 51%; arbitrariness and indiscriminate targeting in 21%; and the victimization of civilians, noncombatants, neutrals, or outsiders in 17.5%."[76] A similar study conducted by Ariel Merari identified three similar characteristics across the legal definitions of terrorism used in Britain, the United States, and Germany: "(1) the use of violence, (2) political objectives, and (3) the aim of propagating fear in a target population."[77]

In *A Practitioner's Way Forward*, David Brannan, Kristin Darken, and Anders Strindberg explain that when looking at the various components of terrorism found in definitions by renowned scholars, terrorism is generally composed of the following essential elements: "The threat or use of force with the intent to influence political or social

---

[73] Morag.

[74] Hoffman, *Inside Terrorism*, 39–40.

[75] Jonathan Matusitz, "What Is Terrorism?" in *Terrorism and Communication: A Critical Introduction* (Thousand Oaks, CA: SAGE, 2013), 2, https://www.sagepub.com/sites/default/files/upm-binaries/51172_ch_1.pdf.

[76] Matusitz, 2.

[77] Matusitz, 2.

situations, by affecting an audience beyond those directly targeted by the violence, and targeting those traditionally perceived as non-combatants in an effort to create fear."[78] Absent a universally accepted definition, and considering that these characteristics are widely found across terrorism literature, the core elements of terrorism as expressed by Brannan, Darken, and Anders are applied throughout the analysis of this thesis.

### b. *Evolution in the Nature of Terrorism*

Another noteworthy aspect of terrorism studies is the evolution in the perceived nature of terrorism. As Bruce Hoffman explains, the term has evolved to acclimate with the politics and discourse of every era.[79] In the 1930s, terrorism involved tactics of mass repression by totalitarian states against their own citizen populations.[80] In the late 1960s and 1970s, terrorism was assessed within a revolutionary context to involve nationalist and ethnic separatist groups like the Palestinian Liberation Organization.[81] With the attacks of September 11, 2001, terrorism shifted to a religious framework.[82] In our present high-tech world, cyberterrorism is considered one of the most significant threats to our national security.[83] Perhaps it is the changing nature of this phenomenon that also gives way to explore a potential nexus between female genital mutilation and terrorism in yet another context—one that involves gender relations.

### D. CHAPTER OVERVIEW

This thesis consists of three additional chapters. Chapter II presents an understanding of female genital mutilation. Chapter III analyzes female genital mutilation

---

[78] Brannan, Darken, and Strindberg, *Terrorism Analysis*, 23.

[79] Hoffman, *Inside Terrorism*, 20.

[80] Hoffman, 14.

[81] Hoffman, 16.

[82] Hoffman, 18.

[83] Larisa Redins, "Understanding Cyberterrorism," *Risk Management* 59, no. 8 (October 2012): 32, http://libproxy.nps.edu/login?url=https://search.proquest.com/docview/1173888997?accountid=12702.

as an act of terrorism and presents a summary of findings. Chapter IV concludes the thesis and provides recommendations.

*This chapter contains images that readers may find disturbing.*

## II. FEMALE GENITAL MUTILATION

In terrorism analysis, it is the occurrence of a specific act—for example, a bombing or airline hijacking—that prompts investigation and examination into whether or not the act equates to terrorism. Therefore, to examine whether or not female genital mutilation is an act of terrorism, this chapter seeks an understanding of the act itself.

### A. BACKGROUND

As described in Chapter I, female genital mutilation involves "the partial or total removal of the external female genitalia, or other injury to the female genital organs" for no medical reason.[84] Many girls experience female genital mutilation before their fifth birthday.[85] In Gambia, Mauritania, and Indonesia, approximately 50 percent of girls between the ages of zero and fourteen are cut.[86] In Yemen, 85 percent of girls are cut within the first week after their birth.[87]

The origin of female genital mutilation is unclear.[88] Much of the research on this topic indicates that it evolved thousands of years ago during early Egyptian civilization as a means of male control over women.[89] Today, female genital mutilation is mostly concentrated in Africa; in countries like Somalia, Guinea, Djibouti, Sierra Leone, Mali,

---

[84] WHO, "Sexual and Reproductive Health."

[85] "Female Genital Mutilation/Cutting: A Global Concern," UNICEF, 2016, https://www.unicef.org/media/files/FGMC_2016_brochure_final_UNICEF_SPREAD.pdf.

[86] UNICEF.

[87] UNICEF.

[88] Nawal M. Nour, "Female Genital Cutting: A Persisting Practice," *Reviews in Obstetrics and Gynecology* 1, no. 3 (2008): 136, https://www.ncbi.nlm.nih.gov/pmc/articles/PMC2582648/pdf/RIOG001003_0135.pdf.

[89] Susan Costello, "Female Genital Mutilation/Cutting: Risk Management and Strategies for Social Workers and Health Care Professionals," *Risk Management and Healthcare Policy* 2015, no. 8 (December 2018): 226, https://doi.org/10.2147/RMHP.S62091.

Egypt, Sudan, and Eritrea, more than 80 percent of the women ages fourteen to fifty-nine have undergone female genital mutilation.[90] It is also prevalent in such areas of the Middle East as Iraq and Yemen, as well as in Asia, particularly in Indonesia.[91]

Because of global migration patterns, female genital mutilation is also currently performed in Europe and in countries like Australia, New Zealand, and the United States by certain immigrant communities who want to continue the practice on their daughters.[92] In the United States, the volume of women and girls at risk widely differs across states.[93] PRB reports that "in 2013, approximately three-fifths of all women and girls at risk" of female genital mutilation resided in eight states: California, Maryland, Minnesota, New Jersey, New York, Texas, Virginia, and Washington.[94]

**B.     TYPES**

The types of female genital mutilation practiced vary based on ethnicity or national origin.[95] In 1997, a joint statement from WHO and nine other organizations that deal with human rights classified the various forms of female genital mutilation into four types (depicted in Figure 1):

> Type I: Partial or total removal of the clitoris and/or the prepuce (clitoridectomy).
>
> Type II: Partial or total removal of the clitoris and the labia minora, with or without excision of the labia majora (excision).
>
> Type III: Narrowing of the vaginal orifice with creation of a covering seal by cutting and appositioning the labia minora and/or the labia majora, with or without excision of the clitoris (infibulation).

---

[90] UNICEF, "Female Genital Mutilation/Cutting: A Global Concern."

[91] UNICEF.

[92] Population Reference Bureau, "Women and Girls at Risk."

[93] Population Reference Bureau.

[94] Population Reference Bureau.

[95] WHO, *Eliminating Female Genital Mutilation*, 10; "Sexual and Reproductive Health."

Type IV: All other harmful procedures to the female genitalia for non-medical purposes, for example: pricking, piercing, incising, scraping and cauterization.[96]

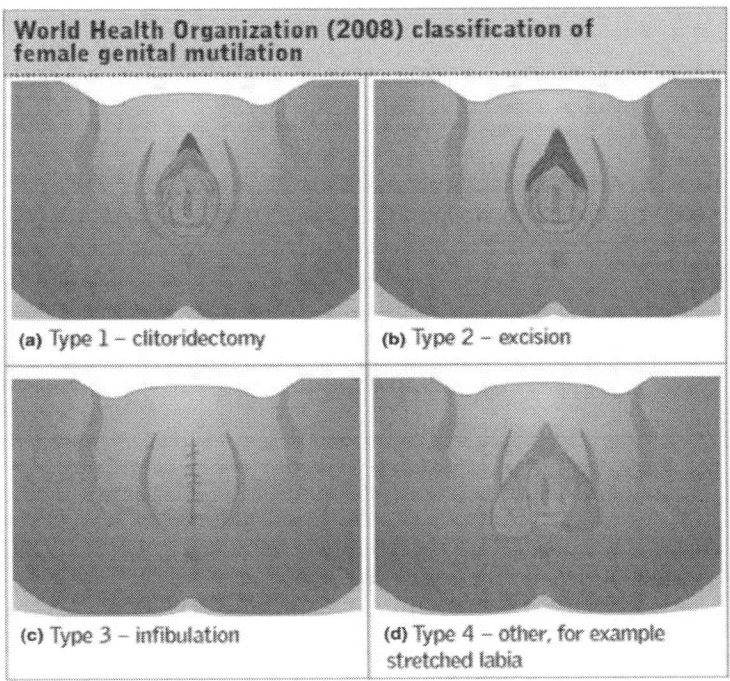

Figure 1. Types of female genital mutilation[97]

Approximately 80 percent of all female genital mutilation procedures involve Type I, clitoridectomy, and Type II, excision (see Figure 2).[98] Both of these types are found in West African countries like Guinea, Mali, and Burkina Faso, where there is a tendency to remove flesh "without sewing the labia minora and/or majora together."[99]

---

[96] WHO, *Eliminating Female Genital Mutilation*, 10.

[97] Source: Khady Diouf and Nawal Nour, "Female Genital Cutting and HIV Transmission: Is There an Association?" *American Journal of Reproductive Immunology* 69, no. 1 (September 2012): 46, https://doi.org/10.1111/aji.12028.

[98] Costello, "Female Genital Mutilation/Cutting," 226.

[99] WHO, "Sexual and Reproductive Health."

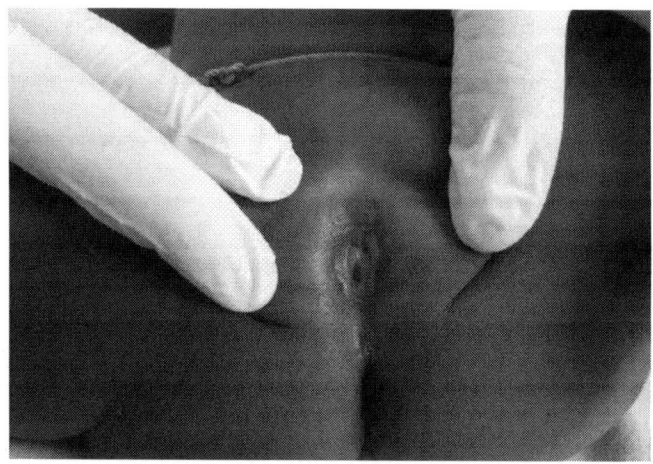

Figure 2. Type II female genital mutilation on a one-year-old girl[100]

Type III, infibulation, is the most severe type of female genital mutilation.[101] When Type III is performed, a girl's legs are typically tied together to keep her from moving for approximately two weeks so scar tissue may form (see Figure 3).[102] The "infibulated scar covers the urethra and most of opening of the introitus [vaginal canal], leaving a small hole for urination and menses" (see Figure 4).[103] Women who undergo infibulation are subjected to "subsequent surgery or cutting (de-infibulation) or other forms of force to open the vagina for sexual intercourse and childbirth."[104] This type of mutilation is largely practiced in the northeast area of Africa to include Ethiopia, Sudan, Eritrea, Djibouti, and Somalia.[105]

---

[100] Source: Kouie Plo et al., "Female Genital Mutilation in Infants and Young Girls: Report of Sixty Cases Observed at the General Hospital of Abobo (Abidjan, Cote D'Ivoire, West Africa)," *International Journal of Pediatrics* (2014): 3, http://dx.doi:10.1155/2014/837471.

[101] United Nations Population Fund, "Female Genital Mutilation."

[102] WHO, "Sexual and Reproductive Health."

[103] Nour, "Female Genital Cutting," 136.

[104] Costello, "Female Genital Mutilation/Cutting," 227.

[105] United Nations Population Fund, "Female Genital Mutilation."

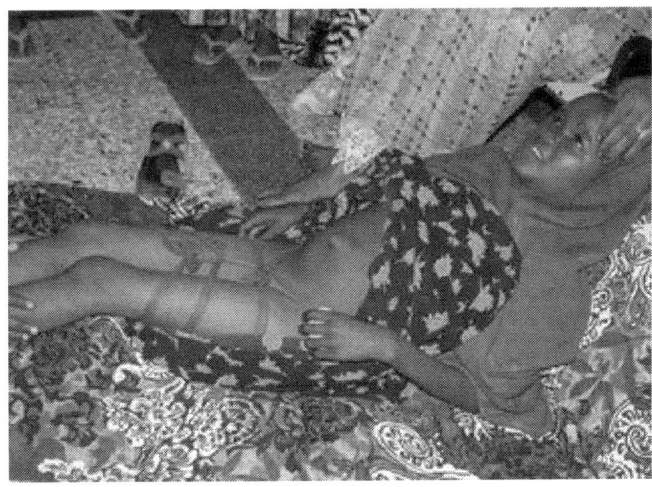

Figure 3. Girl with her legs bound together after Type III infibulation[106]

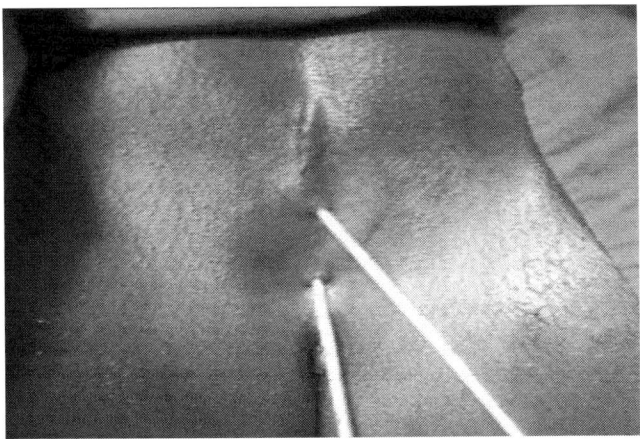

Figure 4. Type III infibulation with the urethral and vaginal orifices[107]

---

[106] Source: Tracy McVeigh and Tara Sutton, "British Girls Undergo Horror of Genital Mutilation Despite Tough Laws," *Guardian*, July 24, 2010, http://www.theguardian.com/society/2010/jul/25/female-circumcision-children-british-law.

[107] Source: İsmail Burak Gültekin et al., "Surgical Reconstruction in Female Genital Mutilation," *Turkish Journal of Urology* 42, no. 2 (2016): 112, https://doi.org/10.5152/tud.2015.89982.

Type IV is performed in areas of Indonesia, India, Israel, Iraq, Malaysia, Thailand, and the United Arab Emirates.[108] According to WHO, there are various forms of Type IV which do not require the removal of genital tissue.[109]

The type of female genital mutilation that is performed in the United States is influenced by the ethnicity of the immigrants who are attempting to sustain the practice. The top ten countries of origin of U.S. women and girls at risk are Egypt, Ethiopia, Somalia, Nigeria, Liberia, Sierra Leone, Sudan, Kenya, Eritrea, and Guinea.[110] Egypt, Ethiopia, and Somalia account for 55 percent of all U.S. women and girls at risk.[111] In Egypt, Types I and II are widely practiced; in Ethiopia and Somalia, Type III, the most severe form, is prevalent.[112]

### C. TERMINOLOGY

The terminology used to reference female genital mutilation has evolved over the years. It was initially called female circumcision, a term criticized in the 1970s by those working to eliminate the practice, as it misleadingly indicates that the practice "is analogous to male circumcision."[113] As a matter of public health and depending on the type that is performed, female genital mutilation is far more severe than male circumcision.[114] Patricia Broussard writes that "a more apt comparison is to compare FGM [female genital mutilation] to castration since the procedure removes a vital part of the

---

[108] Costello, "Female Genital Mutilation/Cutting," 227.

[109] WHO. "Sexual and Reproductive Health."

[110] Population Reference Bureau, "Women and Girls at Risk."

[111] Population Reference Bureau.

[112] "Prevalence of Female Genital Cutting among Egyptian Girls," WHO, accessed July 20, 2018, http://www.who.int/bulletin/volumes/86/4/07-042093/en/; Population Reference Bureau, "Women and Girls at Risk."

[113] UNICEF, *Female Genital Mutilation and Cutting: A Statistical Overview*, 7.

[114] Nahid Toubia, "Female Circumcision as a Public Health Issue," *The New England Journal of Medicine* 331, no. 11 (September 15, 1994): 712, https://www.nejm.org/doi/pdf/10.1056/NEJM199409 153311106.

sexual organ that allows a woman to have orgasm and experience the pleasure associated with intercourse."[115]

To express the differences between male circumcision and the cutting of women's genitalia, many began to apply the term *female genital mutilation* and the acronym FGM.[116] In 1990, the Inter-African Committee on Traditional Practices Affecting the Health of Women and Children adopted the term female genital mutilation. The following year, WHO provided a recommendation to the United Nations to also adopt the term.[117] As some governments and organizations viewed the word *mutilation* as conferring judgment, international development agencies and researchers began to use the term *female genital cutting* (FGC) to be more culturally sensitive.[118] The United States, as well as many international entities, use a hybrid of the term (female genital mutilation/cutting, or FGM/C).[119] According to UNICEF, use of the term mutilation is intended to "highlight that the practice is a violation of the rights of girls and women" and is widely used in various UN and intergovernmental publications.[120]

Throughout this thesis, the practice is referred to as female genital mutilation, without applying the acronym, to place continued emphasis on its damaging effects on women and girls.

### D. TRADITIONAL AND MEDICAL PRACTITIONERS

Despite the health risks and lack of medical necessity associated with the practice, female genital mutilation continues to be performed by both traditional and medical practitioners. As with any terrorism analysis, it is essential to identify the perpetrators of the act and then work toward developing an understanding of their actions and motives in

---

[115] Broussard, "Female Genital Mutilation," 26.

[116] UNICEF, *Female Genital Mutilation and Cutting: A Statistical Overview*, 7.

[117] UNICEF, 7.

[118] UNICEF, 7.

[119] UNICEF, 7; Department of Health and Human Services, "Female Genital Mutilation or Cutting."

[120] UNICEF, *Female Genital Mutilation and Cutting: A Statistical Overview*, 7.

the context in which they took place. In the case of female genital mutilation, the most obvious perpetrators are the individuals who perform the actual cutting.

Generally, traditional practitioners perform female genital mutilation, as depicted in Figure 5.[121] These individuals are commonly community and religious leaders, midwives, and others viewed as "local structures of power and authority."[122] They typically cut the girl's genitalia without anesthesia using unsterile razor blades, scissors, broken glass, and a variety of other crude instruments, some of which are depicted in Figure 6.[123] Once the girl is cut, "sutures, thread, and local concoctions such as oil, honey, dough, or tree sap are used to ease bleeding."[124] In certain regions in West Africa, the practitioners apply dirt, animal feces, or ashes after the procedure to prevent excessive bleeding.[125] Traditional practitioners often travel throughout villages with their instruments to carry out female genital mutilation at the request of parents or other relatives.[126]

---

[121] WHO, "Female Genital Mutilation."

[122] WHO, *Eliminating Female Genital Mutilation*, 6; UNICEF, *Female Genital Mutilation and Cutting: A Statistical Overview*, 42.

[123] Mitchum, "Slapping the Hand of Cultural Relativism," 592; United Nations Population Fund, "Female Genital Mutilation."

[124] Nour, "Female Genital Cutting," 136.

[125] Micthum, "Slapping the Hand of Cultural Relativism," 592.

[126] Nour, "Female Genital Cutting," 136.

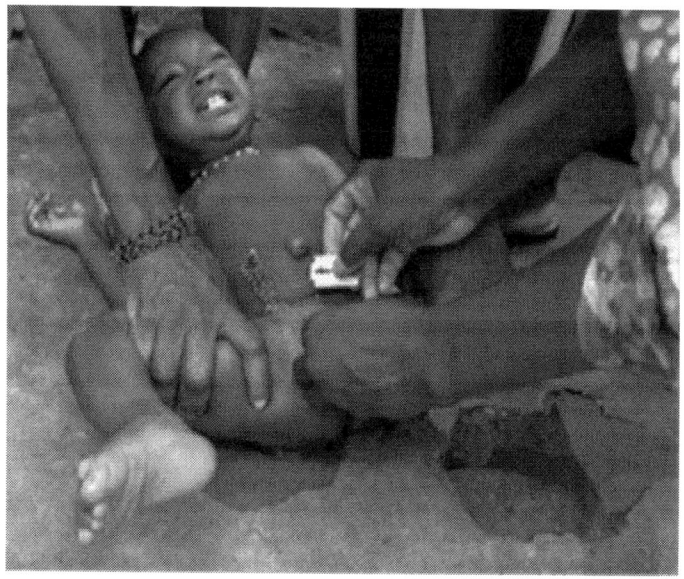

Figure 5. Female genital mutilation performed on a young girl by traditional practitioners[127]

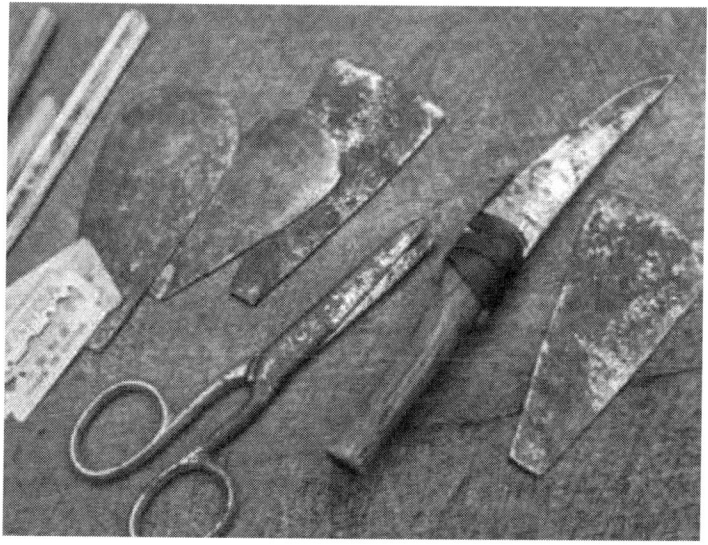

Figure 6. Tools used to perform female genital mutilation[128]

---

[127] Source: Mark Muhama, "Girl, 10, Dies after Female Genital Mutilation in Sierra Leone," *The Weekly Tide*, December 24, 2018, http://theweeklytide.com/2018/12/24/girl-10-dies-after-female-genital-mutilation-in-sierra-leone/.

[128] Source: "The Controversy over Female Genital Cutting," *Encyclopedia Britannica*, accessed January 14, 2018, https://www.britannica.com/story/the-controversy-over-female-genital-cutting.

In some practicing societies, medical practitioners such as doctors and nurses, or other trained health workers, may perform female genital mutilation in their offices using anesthesia.[129] When health-care professionals are involved, this is referred to as the medicalization of female genital mutilation.[130] The United Nations Population Fund (UNFPA) estimates that approximately one out of five girls who has undergone female genital mutilation was cut by a trained health-care professional.[131] This number can average as high as three out of four girls in some countries.[132] UNFPA reports that Sudan, Egypt, Kenya, Guinea, and Nigeria have the highest majority of female genital mutilations performed by medical practitioners.[133]

Some medical professionals promote the medicalization of the procedure as a means to minimize health risks.[134] According to Dr. G. I. Serour of Al-Azhar University in Cairo, however, medicalization does not decrease the long-term complications of the procedure, "has no benefit what so ever, has no medical indication, and thus its performance violates the code of medical ethics."[135]

### E. IMMEDIATE HEALTH COMPLICATIONS AND LONG-TERM CONSEQUENCES

The variety of health complications resulting from female genital mutilation are widely documented in medical journals and generally grouped by immediate and long-term health consequences. The physical and psychological complications that may result vary depending on the type of female genital mutilation performed, the practitioner's skill, the

---

[129] Nour, "Female Genital Cutting," 136.

[130] G.I. Serour, "Medicalization of Female Genital Mutilation/Cutting," *African Journal of Urology* 19, no. 3 (September 2013): 145, https://doi.org/10.1016/j.afju.2013.02.004.

[131] United Nations Population Fund, "Female Genital Mutilation."

[132] United Nations Population Fund.

[133] United Nations Population Fund.

[134] Serour, "Medicalization of Female Genital Mutilation/Cutting," 145.

[135] Serour, 145.

cleanliness of the conditions, and amount of resistance from the girl or woman while she is being cut.[136]

Immediate effects include extreme pain and excessive bleeding as sensitive genital tissue and nerve endings are cut.[137] Infections and the contraction of hepatitis and/or HIV may occur from the use of non-sterile instruments as well as swelling of the genital tissue.[138] Pain and hemorrhaging can also cause girls and women to experience shock.[139] Other immediate health risks include urine retention and infection, ulceration of the genital region, fever, and septicemia.[140]

In the most severe cases, female genital mutilation can lead to death resulting from infections and hemorrhaging.[141] As recent as September 2018, various international media outlets reported the story of a ten-year-old Somali girl named Deeqa Dahir Nuur.[142] While undergoing female genital mutilation in her village, Deeqa suffered from excessive bleeding from a severed vein.[143] She was taken to Dhusmareb Hospital where she later bled to death.[144] Even when performed in a medical setting by health-care practitioners, there is a chance the practice may have a fatal end; in 2016, Mayar Mohamed Mousa, a

---

[136] United Nations Population Fund, "Female Genital Mutilation."

[137] WHO, "Sexual and Reproductive Health."

[138] Serour, "Medicalization of Female Genital Mutilation/Cutting," 146; WHO, "Sexual and Reproductive Health."

[139] WHO, "Sexual and Reproductive Health."

[140] Serour, "Medicalization of Female Genital Mutilation/Cutting," 146.

[141] WHO, "Sexual and Reproductive Health."

[142] May Bulman, "10-Year-Old Girl Bleeds to Death after Undergoing FGM in Somalia," *Independent*, July 21, 2018, https://www.independent.co.uk/news/world/africa/fgm-girl-dies-bleed-death-somalia-olol-galmudug-a8458071.html.

[143] Bulman.

[144] Bulman.

seventeen-year-old girl, died of excessive bleeding while undergoing female genital mutilation in a private hospital in Egypt.[145]

The long-term health consequences also vary and can include chronic pain because of the damage to genital tissue and nerve endings as well as the formation of keloids.[146] Because of the damage to the genital tissue, especially the clitoris, women can experience problems with their sexual health, to include pain during intercourse, difficulty during penetration, inability or reduced frequency of orgasms, and a decrease in sexual desire.[147] According to WHO, "scar formation, pain and traumatic memories associated with the procedure" may also result.[148]

Women may also experience chronic genital and reproductive tract infections, and painful urination due to recurrent urinary tract infections.[149] When Type III female genital mutilation is performed, women often experience menstrual problems with the obstruction of the vaginal opening, which leads to complications in passing menstrual blood.[150] Female genital mutilation can also produce obstetric complications and such perinatal risks as a "higher incident of infant resuscitation at delivery and intrapartum stillbirth and neonatal death."[151] Long-term effects also involve such psychological complications as post-traumatic stress disorder (PTSD), depression, and anxiety disorders.[152]

---

[145] Agence France-Presse, "Egyptian Girl Dies during Female Circumcision Operation," *Telegraph*, May 30, 2016, https://www.telegraph.co.uk/news/2016/05/30/egyptian-girl-dies-during-female-circumcision-operation/; "Female Genital Mutilation is Still Killing Girls in Egypt," Plan International, June 2, 2017, https://plan-international.org/press-releases/female-genital-mutilation-still-killing-girls-egypt.

[146] WHO, "Sexual and Reproductive Health."

[147] WHO.

[148] WHO.

[149] WHO.

[150] WHO.

[151] WHO.

[152] WHO.

Despite no medical need to support the practice, female genital mutilation has been carried out on women for thousands of years. It is the disregard for the bodily integrity of women as well as the severity and enormity of the health consequences described above that distinguish female genital mutilation from male circumcision and have resulted in the international recognition of the practice as a human rights violation.

THIS PAGE INTENTIONALLY LEFT BLANK

*This chapter contains images that readers may find disturbing.*

## III. ANALYSIS

The evolution of female genital mutilation—from a once taboo topic to an internationally recognized human rights violation—has drawn emphasis on its damaging effects to women and girls. In this analysis, female genital mutilation is also examined as an act of terrorism to shed light on how it is used as a violent technique to control women and influence gender inequalities. Through an analysis of the practice against the core characteristics of terrorism, this analysis reveals how female genital mutilation can be classified as an act of terrorism.

### A. DOES FEMALE GENITAL MUTILATION INVOLVE A THREAT OR USE OF FORCE?

As Hoffman explains, "all terrorist acts involve violence or the threat of violence."[153] When reviewing whether female genital mutilation involves a threat or use of force, little analysis is necessary; there is consensus across the literature that the act itself is, de facto, violent in nature.

The practice of female genital mutilation, which has no medical benefit and only causes harm to women, is internationally recognized as an act of violence under the UN framework and violates numerous human rights.[154] Article 2 of the UN General Assembly Resolution 48/10, Declaration on the Elimination of Violence against Women, explains that violence against women is understood to include female genital mutilation.[155] According to UNFPA, statements provided by such bodies as the Committee on the Elimination of Discrimination against Women and Special Rapporteur on violence against

---

[153] Hoffman, *Inside Terrorism*, 40.

[154] United Nations Population Fund, *International and Regional Human Rights Framework*, 30.

[155] United Nations General Assembly, Declaration on the Elimination of Violence against Women (48/104, 85th Plenary Meeting, December 20, 1993), http://www.un.org/documents/ga/res/48/a48r104.htm.

women "give evidence to this fact."[156] UNFPA also emphasizes that "parents, traditional practitioners, medical staff know that they are inflicting pain and that health consequences might be extremely serious."[157]

Personal accounts of women and girls who have undergone female genital mutilation further underscore the violent nature of the practice. Zainab, a woman who underwent female genital mutilation at eight years old along with sisters, shares their experience:

> We fought back; we really thought we were going to die because of the pain. You have one woman holding your mouth so you won't scream, two holding your chest and the other two holding your legs. After we were infibulated, we had rope tied across our legs so it was like we had to learn to walk again. We had to try to go to the toilet. If you couldn't pass water in the next 10 days something was wrong. We were lucky, I suppose. We gradually recovered and didn't die like the other girl. But the memory and the pain never really go away.[158]

Hibo Wardere had female genital mutilation performed on her when she was six years old:

> I got held down by my auntie and the cutter's helper, and my mother was standing there. How I was ripped apart. How I was screaming for dear life and begged, and begged, for mercy. But nobody stopped. Six years old and I actually prayed to die that day. I prayed because the pain was so great it just literally consumed me from head to toe. It was just too much.
>
> The cutter had a horrific razor blade that didn't even look like a razor blade. It had all kinds of shades of brown, you name them, they were on it. They were dirty razors. That is the razor that she will use for 10 or 20 girls that day. No hygiene involved, nothing. No anesthesia at all. You are just butchered. You could see your flesh. You could see your blood all over her hands. It was a complete, utter horrific, nightmare.[159]

---

[156] United Nations Population Fund, *International and Regional Human Rights Framework*, 29.

[157] United Nations Population Fund, 31.

[158] United Nations Population Fund, "Female Genital Mutilation (FGM)."

[159] "'A Horrific Nightmare': Female Genital Mutilation Survivor Shares Her Story in Ottawa," CBC, September 29, 2016, https://www.cbc.ca/radio/asithappens/as-it-happens-thursday-edition-1.3784062/a-horrific-nightmare-female-genital-mutilation-survivor-shares-her-story-in-ottawa-1.3784067.

Author, politician, and women's rights advocate Ayaan Hirsi Ali describes her experience undergoing female genital mutilation as a five-year old girl in Somalia:

> Then scissors went down between my legs and the man cut off my inner labia and clitoris. I heard it, like a butcher snipping the fat off a piece of meat. A piercing pain shot between my legs, indescribable, and I howled. Then came the sewing; the long, blunt needle clumsily pushed into my bleeding outer labia, my loud and angry protests…. When the sewing was finished, the man cut the thread off with his teeth.[160]

These personal accounts of women describe torture. In fact, the UN has provided that female genital mutilation violates the "right not to be subjected to torture," identifying the practice as a form of "cruel, inhuman and degrading treatment."[161]

In sum, female genital mutilation, like terrorism, embodies an act that is forceful and violent. Women and girls are intentionally targeted, on the basis of their gender alone, to undergo a violent procedure that can lead to damaging and lifelong physical and mental health consequences and, in the most severe cases, death.[162]

## B. DOES FEMALE GENITAL MUTILATION INVOLVE AN INTENT TO INFLUENCE POLITICAL OR SOCIAL SITUATIONS?

To determine if female genital mutilation is a violent act carried out with the intent of influencing political or social situations, it is critical to focus on the emic perspective of those who facilitate or perform the procedure.[163] It is therefore essential to examine the motive for cutting women and girls. The most common reasons for practicing female genital mutilation are grouped into five categories: sociocultural, psychosexual, socioeconomic, religious, and hygiene and aesthetics.[164] In light of these reasons, it is

---

[160] Ayaan Hirsi Ali, *Infidel* (New York: Free Press, 2008), 32.

[161] United Nations Population Fund, *International and Regional Human Rights Framework*, 30.

[162] United Nations Population Fund, 31.

[163] Brannan, Darken, and Strindberg, *Terrorism Analysis*, 45.

[164] United Nations Population Fund, "Female Genital Mutilation."

apparent that, much like terrorism is designed to influence social situations, female genital mutilation is largely carried out to adversely influence women's role in society.[165]

### 1. Sociocultural Reasons

For many practicing societies, female genital mutilation serves as a rite of passage to make women and girls eligible for marriage.[166] Khadijah Sharif explains, "[I]n cultures that practice female genital mutilation, the ritual confers upon women full social acceptability, integration into the community, and serves as a rite of passage to womanhood."[167] Once they are cut, girls or women are accepted as full members of their societies and can receive some social privileges and benefits.[168] For instance, in the Sabiny culture in Uganda, women "cannot speak in front of elders, hold any position of responsibility, or even marry" if they have not undergone female genital mutilation.[169]

In communities where female genital mutilation is prevalent, the preservation of honor is another key factor for the continuation of the practice.[170] Honor is strongly "related to acceptable sexual behavior for women."[171] The matter of honor is especially important in communities that are patrilineal, where marriages are viewed as alliances between clans.[172] Uncut women and their families are often considered out-groups and are

---

[165] United Nations Population Fund.

[166] Broussard, "Female Genital Mutilation," 31.

[167] Khadijah Sharif, "Female Genital Mutilation: What Does the New Federal Law Really Mean?" *Forhdam Urban Law Journal* 24, no. 2 (January 1997): 415, https://ir.lawnet.fordham.edu/cgi/viewcontent.cgi?referer=https://www.google.com/&httpsredir=1&article=1963&context=ulj.

[168] Sharif, 415.

[169] Leigh Trueblood, "Female Genital Mutilation: A Discussion of International Human Rights Instruments, Cultural Sovereignty and Dominance Theory," *Denver Journal of International Law and Policy* 28, no. 4 (September 22, 2000), 437.

[170] Osman Mahmoudi and Elham Hosseini, "The Relationship between Honor-Based Violence and Female Genital Mutilation in Janvanrood County," *International Journal of Health and Life Sciences* 4, no. 2 (November 14, 2018): 1, https://doi.org/10.5812/ijhls.83680.

[171] Mahmoudi and Hosseini.

[172] "Female Genital Mutilation: Information for Health and Child Protection Professionals," New Zealand FGM Programme, accessed January 17, 2019, http://fgm.co.nz/beliefs-and-issues/.

shamed and ostracized.[173] Therefore, a girl's mother and relatives may submit the girl to female genital mutilation based on the desire to defend their honor.[174]

Preservation of group identity of the practicing community is also a motivation for the practice.[175] Often the parents of young girls will request female genital mutilation for their daughters because it is supported by the family's community as part of their cultural identity.[176] The effort to safeguard group identity is also demonstrated by the "older women who have themselves been mutilated," who often act as "gatekeepers of the practice, seeing it as essential to the identity of women and girls. This is probably one reason why women, and more often older women, are more likely to support the practice, and tend to see efforts to combat the practice as an attack on their identity and culture."[177]

Nahid Toubia explains that cultural identity is extremely important for groups that experienced colonialism. In Africa, for example, "immigrants are faced with a stronger majority culture, and … change does not favor those holding social power (that is, men.)"[178] In the early 1930s, as Christian colonists attempted to end the practice of female genital mutilation in Kenya, anti-colonial activist and politician Jomo Kenyatta spoke out in support of female genital mutilation, expressing a view that many currently still share:

> [I]t is impossible for a member of the [Kikuyu] tribe to imagine an initiation without clitoridectomy … the abolition of the Irua [the ritual operation] will destroy the tribal symbol which identifies the age group and prevent the

---

[173] UNICEF, *Innocenti Insight: The Dynamics of Social Change towards the Abandonment of Female Genital Mutilation/Cutting in Five African Countries* (Florence, Italy: UNICEF Innocenti Research Center, 2010), https://www.unicef-irc.org/publications/pdf/fgm_insight_eng.pdf.

[174] Mahmoudi and Hosseini, "Honor-Based Violence."

[175] Toubia, "Female Circumcision as a Public Health Issue," 714.

[176] WHO, *Female Genital Mutilation: An Overview* (Geneva, Switzerland: WHO, 1998), 2, http://apps.who.int/iris/bitstream/10665/42042/1/9241561912_eng.pdf.

[177] WHO, *Eliminating Female Genital Mutilation*, 7.

[178] Toubia, "Female Circumcision as a Public Health Issue," 714.

> Kikuya from perpetuating the spirit of collectivism and national solidarity which they have been able to maintain from time immemorial.[179]

According to the International Organization for Migration, when migrant communities face social challenges such as those associated with integration within their new environment, a common outcome is "withdrawal into the community and sometimes stricter application or toughening of cultural practices. In this case, the preservation of ethnic identity is used to mark a distinction from the host society, especially when migrants are resettling in a receiving culture where women have more freedom of choice and expression, including in their sexuality, as compared to their community of origin."[180] WHO further explains that the safeguarding of cultural identity often becomes important to groups during times of extreme social change, such as when they are migrating to another country.[181] For instance, female genital mutilation is practiced by some immigrant communities residing in countries like the United States that have no long-standing tradition of the practice.[182]

### 2. Psychosexual Reasons

Female genital mutilation is also used as a means to control women's sexuality.[183] Practicing societies believe that "women are fundamentally sexual creatures and naturally promiscuous … women are cut to prevent them from succumbing to these impulses."[184] It is the belief that the practice will eliminate or reduce a woman's sexual desires once the

---

[179] Loretta Kopelman, "Female Circumcision/Genital Mutilation and Ethical Relativism," *Second Opinion* 20, no. 2 (October 1994): 62.

[180] "Supporting the Abandonment of Female Genital Mutilation in the Context of Migration," International Organization for Migration, accessed February 23, 2019, https://www.iom.int/jahia/webdav/shared/shared/mainsite/projects/documents/fgm_infosheet.pdf.

[181] WHO, *Eliminating Female Genital Mutilation*, 7.

[182] WHO, 7.

[183] Ibrahim Asmani and Maryam Abdi, *De-linking Female Genital Mutilation/Cutting from Islam* (Washington, DC: USAID, 2008), 24, https://www.unfpa.org/sites/default/files/pub-pdf/De-linking%20 FGM%20from%20Islam%20final%20report.pdf.

[184] Trueblood, "Female Genital Mutilation," 437.

sensitive tissue of the genitalia, for example the clitoris, is cut or removed, and that sexual pleasure will be enhanced for men.[185]

Once submitted to female genital mutilation, women are believed to then be able to remain virgins before marriage and to be faithful during marriage.[186] The link between the practice and virginity is so powerful that a girl who has not been cut has little to no prospect of marriage.[187] A potential bride must often allow the groom or his family to examine her genitalia to ensure she underwent the procedure in order to ascertain her virginity.[188] Toubia also explains that female genital mutilation "is the physical marking of the marriageability of women, because it symbolizes social control of their sexual pleasure."[189]

Along with acting a deterrent to promiscuity, female genitalia are also cut to "reduce a woman's sex drive so the husband can match his wife's when he gets older."[190] A male member of the Sabiny culture explains:

> [M]en used to hunt and whenever they left women behind, they were always uncertain of their faith towards going around with other men. To control this, they started circumcising their women. When that thing [the clitoris] is removed, there is a difference. If not removed, the woman will sleep with other men or not allow the husband to sleep. This can cause friction in the home because after a day's work, a man needs to have enough rest. So the woman must be circumcised to reduce her sexual urge.[191]

---

[185] Trueblood, 437; New Zealand FGM Programme, "Female Genital Mutilation."

[186] Trueblood, "Female Genital Mutilation," 437.

[187] New Zealand FGM Programme, "Female Genital Mutilation."

[188] Sharif, "Female Genital Mutilation," 416.

[189] Toubia, "Female Circumcision as a Public Health Issue," 714.

[190] Mitchum, "Slapping the Hand of Cultural Relativism," 595.

[191] Trueblood, "Female Genital Mutilation," 437.

In societies where men have multiple wives, it is believed that female genital mutilation must be performed to make women less sexually demanding because it is physically impossible for men to satisfy each of their wives.[192]

### 3. Socioeconomic Reasons

Female genital mutilation is also carried out for socioeconomic reasons.[193] It often serves as a source of income for traditional and medical practitioners.[194] The fees can be substantial for practitioners, particularly in countries where the practice is criminalized.[195]

Throughout many practicing communities, women often rely on men for their economic security; therefore, their eligibility to marry is essential.[196] Where female genital mutilation is prevalent, "resources and power are passed down and held solely under male control, with a woman's access to land and to economic resources being exclusively through her husband" or other male relatives.[197]

### 4. Religious Reasons

Although female genital mutilation "has been reported to be practiced by followers of many different religions: Muslims, Catholics, Jews, Animists and Christian Coptics," religious scholars explain that the practice is not supported by any of the religious texts and predates both Islam and Christianity.[198] The religious requirement associated with female genital mutilation is explained across literature as "an incorrect interpretation and teaching

---

[192] New Zealand FGM Programme, "Female Genital Mutilation."

[193] WHO. "Female Genital Mutilation."

[194] Serour, "Medicalization of Female Genital Mutilation/Cutting," 147.

[195] Serour, 145.

[196] New Zealand FGM Programme, "Female Genital Mutilation."

[197] New Zealand FGM Programme.

[198] New Zealand FGM Programme.

of religious texts"; the belief that it is based on religious obligations has reinforced the continuation of the practice.[199]

Although female genital mutilation is widely thought to be required by Islam because it is performed across many Muslim populations, authors Ibrahim Asmani and Maryam Abdi of *De-linking Female Genital Mutilation/Cutting from Islam* explain that the practice is "erroneously seen as a way of complying with the Islamic requirement of chastity and morality."[200] For example, some Muslims believe that if girls "are not cut they will be sexually uncontrollable."[201] This belief was expressed during a video lecture in 2017 by Imam Shaker Elsayed of the Dar Al-Hijrah Islamic Center in Falls Church, Virginia.[202] In the video, Elsayed refers to female genital mutilation as the cutting of "the tip of the sexually sensitive part of the girl so that she is not hypersexually active." He also states that "in societies where circumcision of girls is completely prohibited, hypersexuality takes over the entire society and a woman is not satisfied with one person or two or three."[203]

Despite the beliefs shared by some Muslim communities that maintain the practice, there are no verses within the Quran that require or mention female genital mutilation.[204] Therefore, with no religious authority found in the Quran or any other holy texts supporting it, female genital mutilation is not a religious practice, but rather a cultural one.[205]

---

[199] Broussard, "Female Genital Mutilation," 31.

[200] United Nations Population Fund, "Female Genital Mutilation"; Asmani and Abdi, *De-linking Female Genital Mutilation/Cutting from Islam*, 8.

[201] Asmani and Abdi, *De-linking Female Genital Mutilation/Cutting from Islam*, 8.

[202] Abigail Hauslohner, "A Virginia Imam Said Female Genital Mutilation Prevents 'Hypersexuality,' Leading to Calls for His Dismissal," *Washington Post*, June 5, 2017, https://www.washingtonpost.com/news/acts-of-faith/wp/2017/06/05/virginia-mosque-embattled-after-imam-said-female-genital-mutilation-prevents-hypersexuality/?noredirect=on&utm_term=.82cf7f19d3c5.

[203] Hauslohner.

[204] Asmani and Abdi, *De-linking Female Genital Mutilation/Cutting from Islam*, 17.

[205] United Nations Population Fund, "Female Genital Mutilation."

### 5. Hygiene and Aesthetic Reasons

Women and girls are also cut based on views that females are not attractive or clean until their genitalia are cut.[206] Some share the belief that by cutting the clitoris, unpleasant female odors will be eliminated.[207] Within Somalia, practicing communities view the external genitalia as unclean.[208] The Mosi of Burkina Faso and the Bambara and Dogon of Mali believe the clitoris can cause harm to a baby during childbirth.[209]

Some also view the clitoris as unfeminine.[210] Certain groups in Sudan believe "that the clitoris will grow until it dangles between the legs, in rivalry with the male penis, if not cut."[211] Therefore, female genital mutilation is also performed to prevent challenges to male authority with respect to the size of genitalia.[212]

### 6. Summary of Reasons

Upon review of the five primary reasons cited for female genital mutilation, as well as various rationale under each motive, there are instances that convey the procedure is widely used to influence social situations. A summation of the primary reasons to practice female genital mutilation linked to instances where there is intent to influence social situations is provided in Table 1.

---

[206] WHO, "Female Genital Mutilation."

[207] Mitchum, "Slapping the Hand of Cultural Relativism," 595.

[208] New Zealand FGM Programme, "Female Genital Mutilation."

[209] New Zealand FGM Programme.

[210] WHO. "Female Genital Mutilation."

[211] Broussard, "Female Genital Mutilation," 26.

[212] Broussard, 33.

Table 1. Primary reasons for the practice of female genital mutilation and their link to intent to influence political or social situations

| Reason | Intent to Influence Political or Social Situations |
|---|---|
| Sociocultural | To preserve and defend cultural identity and family honor |
| Psychosexual | To control women's sexuality and maintain that only women who have undergone the practice are eligible to marry |
| Socioeconomic | To ensure women's economic dependence on men |
| Aesthetics | To prevent challenges to male authority |

Note: Religion is omitted from the chart, as female genital mutilation is not a supported in any of the religious texts and is therefore a cultural—rather than religious—practice.

Examples of instances when female genital mutilation is not designed to influence social situations involve hygienic reasons or circumstances when it is carried out solely for personal financial gain. However, there is overwhelming evidence that female genital mutilation is used to influence social situations by affecting how society views and treats women.

### C. DOES FEMALE GENITAL MUTILATION AFFECT AN AUDIENCE BEYOND THOSE DIRECTLY TARGETED BY TARGETING THOSE TRADITIONALLY PERCEIVED AS NON-COMBATANTS, IN AN EFFORT TO CREATE FEAR?

Targets of terrorist attacks are perceived as non-combatants and are generally "vulnerable as part of an effort to expose the enemy's inability to defend itself."[213] Targets of female genital mutilation are women and girls. In the societies where female genital mutilation is practiced, women and girls already have little to no power and are likely the most vulnerable members of their communities. Yet, to function as a form of terrorism, female genital mutilation must also affect an audience beyond the target. Brannan, Darken, and Strindberg explain that for terrorism to work properly, it must take the form of a public proclamation "where it can be perceived, assessed, and evaluated by a target audience."[214]

---

[213] Brannan, Darken, and Strindberg, *Terrorism Analysis*, 72.

[214] Brannan, Darken, and Strindberg, 71.

Female genital mutilation is carried out in a variety of settings, some private and others public, as illustrated by the photographs in Figures 7 through 13. When performed privately by a traditional practitioner, a health-care professional in a medical facility, or in someone's home by a village midwife, the practice may appear not to rise to the level of terrorism, but the act is not confined to the space where the cutting is performed. Rather, the action is publicly mediated by those not involved in the violence as a gateway to allow or disallow women access to societal structures. When part of a public ceremony or celebration, female genital mutilation is more clearly perceived as a form of terrorism, given that terrorism functions as a public proclamation.

Figure 7. A Kurdish girl—whose mother tells her she is going to a party—is taken to her neighbor's house where a midwife cuts her genitalia while other girls wait outside to undergo the same[215]

---

[215] Source: Amit Paley, "Widespread Female Circumcision Highlights the Plight of Kurdish Women," *Washington Post*, December 29, 2008, www.washingtonpost.com/wp-dyn/content/article/2008/12/28/AR2008122802005.html?wprss=rss_world.

Figure 8. In Uganda, people gather around girls of the Sebei tribe who have just undergone female genital mutilation[216]

Figure 9. Pokot girls in Kenya seated on rocks during a ceremony for female genital mutilation[217]

---

[216] Photo credit: Reuters/James Akena. Source: Emma Batha, "UN Study Finds More Women Face Genital Mutilation than Estimated," Yahoo!, February 5, 2016, https://news.yahoo.com/un-study-finds-more-women-face-genital-mutilation-081601734.html.

[217] Source: "How Practices and Meaning of FGM Are Changing Tanzania, *The Star*, April 19, 2018, https://www.the-star.co.ke/news/2018/04/19/how-practices-and-meaning-of-fgm-are-changing-in-tanzania_c1746279.

In Sierra Leone, female genital mutilation is orchestrated and performed by the Bondo Society as a rite of passage into womanhood (see Figure 10).[218] The Bondo is a secret, all-women society, "which girls join to become recognized as a woman in her community and which also creates a women-only space for belonging and sisterhood."[219] A ceremony, lasting for several weeks, is planned around the cutting of the girls' genitalia.[220] After the girls are cut, they "are recognized women in their communities" and "led back in procession and dance to the village to be welcomed by their families with gifts and festivities."[221]

Figure 10. Female genital mutilation ceremony in Sierra Leone[222]

---

[218] Owolabi Bjälkander, "Female Genital Mutilation in Sierra Leone" (thesis, Karolinska Institutet, 2013), 13, https://openarchive.ki.se/xmlui/bitstream/handle/10616/41373/Thesis_Owolabi_Bjalkander.pdf?sequence=4&isAllowed=y.

[219] Bjälkander, 13.

[220] Bjälkander, 13.

[221] Bjälkander, 14.

[222] Source: Alusine Sesay, "Sierra Leone: Government Accused of Being Silent about Combating FGM," *Medium*, February 7, 2017, https://medium.com/@premiernews140/sierra-leone-government-accused-of-being-silent-about-combating-fgm-3188c7b292ec.

In Indonesia, female genital mutilation can occur in various settings.[223] Sometimes it is performed in the girl's home where a celebration takes place that day "to mark the girl as a more complete Muslim."[224] When performed at a medical facility, a celebration usually takes place within a week.[225] In the Gorontalo province, girls undergo genital mutilation prior to their third birthday "in a special ceremony known as 'mongubingu' to prove their compliance to Islam" (see Figure 11).[226] Journalist Abigail Haworth reported on mass ceremonies held in Bandung, Indonesia, where large numbers of girls are cut.[227] According to Haworth, an Islamic Foundation in Indonesia known as Yayasan Assalaam coordinates the mass ceremonies "in the lunar month of the Prophet Muhammad's birthday, and pays parents 80,000 rupiah and a bag of food for each daughter they bring to be cut."[228] When Haworth asked Yayasan Assalaam's social welfare secretary why the practice is performed, he replied that it is a requirement to "control women's sexual urges."[229]

---

[223] Reyhana Patel and Khalid Roy, *Female Cutting in Indonesia: A Field Study* (Burlington, ON: Islamic Relief Canada, 2013), 10, http://islamicreliefcanada.org/wp-content/uploads/2016/04/IRC_FGC_Report.pdf.

[224] Patel and Roy, 10.

[225] Patel and Roy, 10.

[226] Purniya Awan, "With No Medical Reasons or Links to Religion, Why Are Women Still Being Circumcised?" *The Express Tribune Blogs*, April 3, 2017, https://blogs.tribune.com.pk/story/48320/with-no-medical-reasons-or-links-to-religion-why-are-women-still-being-circumcised/.

[227] Abigail Haworth, "The Day I Saw 248 Girls Suffering Genital Mutilation," *Guardian*, November 17, 2012, https://www.theguardian.com/society/2012/nov/18/female-genital-mutilation-circumcision-indonesia.

[228] Haworth.

[229] Haworth.

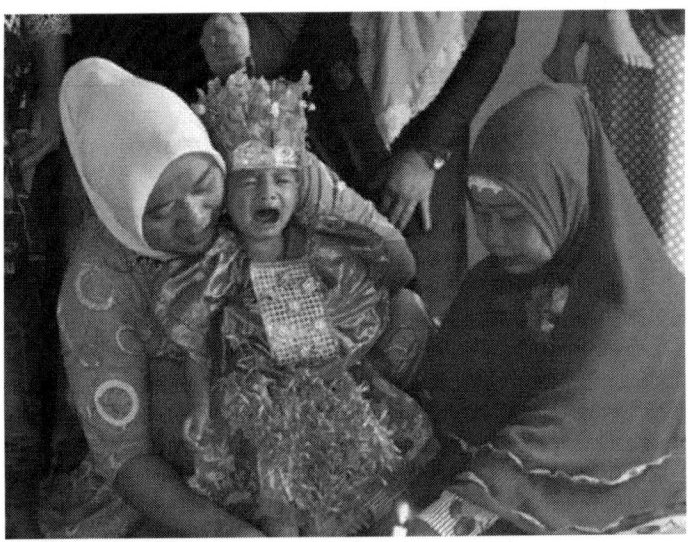

Photo credit: Getty.

Figure 11. Female genital mutilation ceremony in the Gorontalo province of Indonesia[230]

In Kenya and Tanzania, the Kuria people perform female genital mutilation every two years as part of a special ceremony.[231] Arrangements are made in advance while invitations are prepared by family members of the girls that will be cut.[232] On the day of the procedure, girls are taken to a site that is specially prepared for the cutting.[233] Each girl is seated and then held down as the practitioner cuts off her labia minora while singing takes place.[234] The songs that are sung during the ceremonies often include language that portrays the subordination of women and domination by men.[235] As depicted in Figure 12,

---

[230] Source: Awan, "No Medical Reasons."

[231] Joyce Wambura, "Masculinities and Femininities in Female Genital Mutilation Ceremonies in Kuria, Kenya," *Culture, Society and Masculinities* 8, no. 2 (October 1, 2016): 120, https://doi.org/10.3149/CSM.0802.118.

[232] Wambura, 120.

[233] Wambura, 120.

[234] Wambura, 120.

[235] Wambura, 120.

after they are cut, the girls are paraded to their homes, where they are presented with gifts from family and friends.[236]

Figure 12. Kuria girls in Kenya being paraded after undergoing female genital mutilation[237]

The ceremonies associated with female genital mutilation and the celebrations of the actual cutting are used to convey to the rest of society that patriarchy and domination must be accepted either willingly or through force. The social sanctions for not submitting to the practice influence individuals to support female genital mutilation "out of fear of punishment or out of a desire to please and thus be rewarded."[238] Although there are instances where community members have successfully initiated efforts to combat the practice, those who challenge it generally "face condemnation, harassment, and ostracism."[239] The public ceremonies and celebrations surrounding female genital

---

[236] Wambura, 120.

[237] Source: Rachel Horner, "FGM in Kenya: Girls Are Being Paraded Openly in the Streets," *Guardian*, December 23, 2016, https://www.theguardian.com/society/2016/dec/23/fgm-in-kenya-girls-are-being-paraded-openly-in-the-streets.

[238] WHO, *Eliminating Female Genital Mutilation*, 5.

[239] WHO, 5.

mutilation ultimately serve as a means to reinforce the expectations, behavior, and roles of women and, in doing so, have an influential impact on society.

### D. SUMMARY OF FINDINGS

Terrorism is a violent act that is carried out to "influence political or social situations by affecting an audience beyond those directly targeted by the violence … in an effort to create fear."[240] A basic assessment of female genital mutilation against the core characteristics of terrorism reveals that in many instances, all the elements commonly accepted by scholars who study terrorism are found within female genital mutilation. Not all instances of female genital mutilation may meet the criteria for terrorism, but most instances of female genital mutilation addressed in this thesis do.

Ultimately, the practice serves as a violent means to control the female segment of the population and maintain gender inequality. Female genital mutilation affects an audience beyond the girl or woman being cut; in many cases, the violence has been ritualized for public display. While the threat and use of violence does not manifest as a gun or a bomb, the very personal invasion of the body through which it does manifest, including the dishonor and social sanctions that come from not complying, is just as real and devastating.

---

[240] Brannan, Darken, and Strindberg, *Terrorism Analysis*, 43.

## IV. CONCLUSION AND RECOMMENDATIONS

Although the hands that perform and facilitate female genital mutilation seem very different from the hands that have committed acts of terrorism under names like ISIS, Hezbollah, or the Ku Klux Klan, this thesis demonstrates that female genital mutilation can function as a form of terrorism. Specifically, the practice can serve as a form of gender-based terrorism. Religious, political, cyber, and bioterrorism, among others, are provided as classifications of terrorism, yet there is no classification extended to violent acts that specifically target women, including female genital mutilation. As Hoffman explains, the types of terrorism that have surfaced throughout history have evolved to acclimate to the politics and discourse of every era.[241] By demonstrating how female genital mutilation can function as a form of terrorism, this thesis offers another category for experts to explore in the evolution of terrorism: gender-based terrorism.

During the development of this thesis, the federal statute criminalizing female genital mutilation was ruled as unconstitutional.[242] On November 20, 2018, a federal judge dismissed charges on the very first federal case involving two doctors and one co-conspirator in Michigan for cutting the genitalia of girls approximately six to eight years old.[243] Charges were also filed against the mothers for arranging the procedure and transporting their daughters across state lines to Michigan, which at the time did not have laws against female genital mutilation.[244] The judge ruled that Congress lacked authority to criminalize female genital mutilation in the first place, which he deemed a "local criminal activity which, in keeping with long-standing tradition and our federal system of

---

[241] Hoffman, *Inside Terrorism*, 20.

[242] Tresa Baldas, "Judge Dismissed Female Genital Mutilation Charges in Historic Case," Detroit Free Press, November 20, 2018, https://www.freep.com/story/news/local/michigan/detroit/2018/11/20/female-genital-mutilation-michigan/1991712002/.

[243] "Three Indicted for Female Genital Mutilation," U.S. Department of Justice, April 26, 2017, https://www.justice.gov/usao-edmi/pr/three-indicted-female-genital-mutilation.

[244] Emilio Rosenthal, "Anti-FGM Legislation Is Not an Unconstitutional Measure," *The McGill International Review*, January 14, 2019, https://www.mironline.ca/anti-fgm-legislation-is-not-an-unconstitutional-measure.

government, is for the states to regulate, not Congress."[245] The U.S. government filed a notice of appeal on December 19, 2018, of the judge's ruling. The appeal is currently pending.[246]

If the judge's 2018 ruling in the Michigan case is upheld and the matter of legislating female genital mutilation rests with the states, the situation remains unsettled; there are presently twenty-two states without laws criminalizing the practice.[247] Therefore, to protect girls and bring perpetrators to justice, legislators at the state level must act quickly to enact laws where there are none and to strengthen laws that are inadequate.

In this connection, the proposals for state legislation provided by the AHA Foundation appear to be the most impactful for strengthening the legal framework to address female genital mutilation in the United States. AHA recommends laws that:

- Prosecute practitioners, parents and guardians and prosecute for facilitating female genital mutilation

- Increase the penalty above the five year federal penalty

- Criminalize vacation cutting

- Clarify that culture cannot be used as a defense for performing female genital mutilation

- Include education and outreach provisions

- Require professional service providers to report known or suspected instances of female genital mutilation to law enforcement

- Require training for law enforcement professionals[248]

---

[245] Baldas, "Judge Dismissed Female Genital Mutilation Charges."

[246] Virginia Gordan, "Feds to Appeal Decision to Dismiss Charges in Detroit-Area Female Genital Mutilation Case," Michigan Radio, December 20, 2018, http://www.michiganradio.org/post/feds-appeal-decision-dismiss-charges-detroit-area-female-genital-mutilation-case.

[247] "AHA Foundation, "FGM Legislation by State."

[248] "Why We Hesitate to Protect Girls from FGM in the United States," AHA Foundation, updated January 2019, https://www.theahafoundation.org/wp-content/uploads/2019/01/MEDIA-REPORT_AH_RGB_REVISED1.20.pdf.

By revealing how female genital mutilation embodies the core elements of terrorism, this thesis should grant U.S. elected officials a greater sense of urgency to address this problem by strengthening the legal framework against it.

If the United States does not act quickly to protect girls from female genital mutilation, what does this indifference say about the value that is placed on girls in our society? The findings of this thesis should implore state legislators to take immediate action to enact laws that bring perpetrators to justice and safeguard girls from female genital mutilation. Female genital mutilation does more than violate human rights; it can serve as a form of gender-based terrorism against women. Why are we waiting?

THIS PAGE INTENTIONALLY LEFT BLANK

# LIST OF REFERENCES

AHA Foundation. "FGM Legislation by State." Accessed July 29, 2018. https://www.theahafoundation.org/female-genital-mutilation/fgm-legislation-by-state/.

———. "Vacation Cutting: An Illegal Practice Still Running Rampant." Accessed July 29, 2018. https://www.theahafoundation.org/vacation-cutting-an-illegal-practice-still-running-rampant.

———. "Why We Hesitate to Protect Girls from FGM in the United States." Updated January 2019. https://www.theahafoundation.org/wp-content/uploads/2019/01/MEDIA-REPORT_AH_RGB_REVISED1.20.pdf.

Ali, Ayaan Hirsi. *Infidel*. New York: Free Press, 2008.

Asmani, Ibrahim, and Maryam Abdi. *De-linking Female Genital Mutilation/Cutting from Islam*. Washington, DC: USAID, 2008. https://www.unfpa.org/sites/default/files/pub-pdf/De-linking%20FGM%20from%20Islam%20final%20report.pdf.

Awan, Purniya. "With No Medical Reasons or Links to Religion, Why Are Women Still Being Circumcised?" *The Express Tribune Blogs*, April 3, 2017. https://blogs.tribune.com.pk/story/48320/with-no-medical-reasons-or-links-to-religion-why-are-women-still-being-circumcised/.

Baldas, Tresa. "Judge Dismissed Female Genital Mutilation Charges in Historic Case." Detroit Free Press, November 20, 2018. https://www.freep.com/story/news/local/michigan/detroit/2018/11/20/female-genital-mutilation-michigan/1991712002/.

Bale, Jeffrey M., and Gary Ackerman. *Recommendations on the Development of Methodologies and Attributes for Assessing Terrorist Threats of WMD Terrorism*. Monterey, CA: Monterey Institute of International Studies. https://courses.cs.washington.edu/courses/csep590/05au/readings/Bale_Ackerman_FinalReport.pdf.

Batha, Emma. "UN Study Finds More Women Face Genital Mutilation Than Estimated." Yahoo!, February 5, 2016. https://news.yahoo.com/un-study-finds-more-women-face-genital-mutilation-081601734.html.

Bjälkander, Owolabi. "Female Genital Mutilation in Sierra Leone." Thesis, Karolinska Institutet, 2013. https://openarchive.ki.se/xmlui/bitstream/handle/10616/41373/Thesis_Owolabi_Bjalkander.pdf?sequence=4&isAllowed=y.

Brannan, David, Kristin Darken, and Anders Strindberg. *A Practitioner's Way Forward: Terrorism Analysis*. Salinas, CA: Agile Press, 2014.

Broussard, Patricia A. "Female Genital Mutilation: Exploring Strategies for Ending Ritualized Torture; Shaming, Blaming, and Utilizing the Convention against Torture." *Duke Journal of Gender Law and Policy* 15, no. 19 (2008): 19–48. https://scholarship.law.duke.edu/djglp/vol15/iss2/2.

Bulman, May. "10-Year-Old Girl Bleeds to Death after Undergoing FGM in Somalia." *Independent*, July 21, 2018. https://www.independent.co.uk/news/world/africa/fgm-girl-dies-bleed-death-somalia-olol-galmudug-a8458071.html.

CBC. "'A Horrific Nightmare': Female Genital Mutilation Survivor Shares Her Story in Ottawa." September 29, 2016. https://www.cbc.ca/radio/asithappens/as-it-happens-thursday-edition-1.3784062/a-horrific-nightmare-female-genital-mutilation-survivor-shares-her-story-in-ottawa-1.3784067.

Center for Reproductive Rights. "Legislation on Female Genital Mutilation in the United States." Briefing paper, Center for Reproductive Rights, November 2014. https://www.reproductiverights.org/sites/default/files/documents/pub_bp_fgmlawsusa.pdf.

Costello, Susan. "Female Genital Mutilation/Cutting: Risk Management and Strategies for Social Workers and Health Care Professionals." *Risk Management and Healthcare Policy* 2015, no. 8 (December 2018): 225–33. https://doi.org/10.2147/RMHP.S62091.

Diouf, Khady, and Nawal Nour. "Female Genital Cutting and HIV Transmission: Is There an Association?" *American Journal of Reproductive Immunology* 69, no. 1 (September 2012): 45–50. https://doi.org/10.1111/aji.12028.

Equality Now. "What International Human Rights Law Says about Female Genital Mutilation." Accessed February 7, 2019. https://d3n8a8pro7vhmx.cloudfront.net/equalitynow/pages/265/attachments/original/1527182447/FGM_Under_International_Law_EN.pdf?1527182447

France-Presse, Agence. "Egyptian Girl Dies during Female Circumcision Operation." *Telegraph*, May 30, 2016. https://www.telegraph.co.uk/news/2016/05/30/egyptian-girl-dies-during-female-circumcision-operation/

Goldberg, Howard, Paul Stupp, Ekwutosi Okoroh, Ghenet Besera, David Goodman, and Isabella Danel. "Women and Girls at Risk for Genital Mutilation in the U.S." *Public Health Reports* 131, no. 2 (March–April 2016): 340–47. https://doi.org/10.1177/003335491613100218.

Gordan, Virginia. "Feds to Appeal Decision to Dismiss Charges in Detroit-Area Female Genital Mutilation Case." Michigan Radio, December 20, 2018. http://www.michiganradio.org/post/feds-appeal-decision-dismiss-charges-detroit-area-female-genital-mutilation-case.

Gültekin, İsmail Burak, Orhan Altınboğa, Rıza Dur, Osman Kara, and Tuncay Küçüközkan. "Surgical Reconstruction in Female Genital Mutilation." *Turkish Journal of Urology* 42, no. 2 (2016): 112–14. https://doi.org/10.5152/tud.2015.89982.

Hauslohner, Abigail. "A Virginia Imam Said Female Genital Mutilation Prevents 'Hypersexuality,' Leading to Calls for His Dismissal." *Washington Post*, June 5, 2017. https://www.washingtonpost.com/news/acts-of-faith/wp/2017/06/05/virginia-mosque-embattled-after-imam-said-female-genital-mutilation-prevents-hypersexuality/?noredirect=on&utm_term=.82cf7f19d3c5.

Haworth, Abigail. "The Day I Saw 248 Girls Suffering Genital Mutilation." *Guardian*, November 17, 2012. https://www.theguardian.com/society/2012/nov/18/female-genital-mutilation-circumcision-indonesia.

Hoffman, Bruce. *Inside Terrorism*. New York: Columbia University Press, 2006.

Horner, Rachel. "FGM in Kenya: Girls Are Being Paraded Openly in the Streets." *Guardian*, December 23, 2016. https://www.theguardian.com/society/2016/dec/23/fgm-in-kenya-girls-are-being-paraded-openly-in-the-streets.

International Organization for Migration. "Supporting the Abandonment of Female Genital Mutilation in the Context of Migration." Accessed February 23, 2019. https://www.iom.int/jahia/webdav/shared/shared/mainsite/projects/documents/fgm_infosheet.pdf.

Kopelman, Loretta. "Female Circumcision/Genital Mutilation and Ethical Relativism." *Second Opinion* 20, no. 2 (October 1994): 62.

Mahmoudi, Osman, and Elham Hosseini. "The Relationship between Honor-Based Violence and Female Genital Mutilation in Janvanrood County." *International Journal of Health and Life Sciences* 4, no. 2 (November 14, 2018): 1–3. https://doi.org/10.5812/ijhls.83680.

Matusitz, Jonathan. "What Is Terrorism?" In *Terrorism and Communication: A Critical Introduction*. Thousand Oaks, CA: SAGE, 2013. https://www.sagepub.com/sites/default/files/upm-binaries/51172_ch_1.pdf.

McVeigh, Tracy, and Tara Sutton. "British Girls Undergo Horror of Genital Mutilation Despite Tough Laws." *Guardian*, July 24, 2010. http://www.theguardian.com/society/2010/jul/25/female-circumcision-children-british-law.

Mitchum, Preston. "Slapping the Hand of Cultural Relativism: Female Genital Mutilation, Male Dominance, and Health as a Human Rights Framework." *William & Mary Journal of Women and the Law* 19, no. 3 (2013): 585–607. http://scholarship.law.wm.edu/wmjowl/vol19/iss3/4.

Morag, Nadav. "Introduction to Terrorism: Typology, Targets and Organization." Lecture, Naval Postgraduate School Center for Homeland Defense and Security, Monterey, CA, April 2015. https://www.chds.us/coursefiles/comp/lectures/NS3028_Intro_to_Terrorism_v02/player.html.

Muhama, Mark. "Girl, 10, Dies after Female Genital Mutilation in Sierra Leone." *The Weekly Tide*, December 24, 2018. http://theweeklytide.com/2018/12/24/girl-10-dies-after-female-genital-mutilation-in-sierra-leone/.

Muthumbi, Jane, Joar Svaneymyr, Elisa Scolaro, Marleen Temmerman, and Lale Say. "Female Genital Mutilation: A Literature Review of the Current Status of Legislation and Policies in 27 African Countries and Yemen." *African Journal of Reproductive Health* 19, no. 3 (September 2015): 32–40. https://www.ajol.info/index.php/ajrh/article/view/124907/114424.

New Zealand FGM Programme. "Female Genital Mutilation: Information for Health and Child Protection Professionals." Accessed January 17, 2019. http://fgm.co.nz/beliefs-and-issues/.

Nour, Nawal M. "Female Genital Cutting: A Persisting Practice." *Reviews in Obstetrics and Gynecology* 1, no. 3 (2008): 135–39. https://www.ncbi.nlm.nih.gov/pmc/articles/PMC2582648/pdf/RIOG001003_0135.pdf.

Paley, Amit. "Widespread Female Circumcision Highlights the Plight of Kurdish Women." *Washington Post*, December 29, 2008. www.washingtonpost.com/wp-dyn/content/article/2008/12/28/AR2008122802005.html?wprss=rss_world.

Patel, Reyhana, and Khalid Roy. *Female Cutting in Indonesia: A Field Study*. Burlington, ON: Islamic Relief Canada, 2013. http://islamicreliefcanada.org/wp-content/uploads/2016/04/IRC_FGC_Report.pdf.

Plan International. "Female Genital Mutilation is Still Killing Girls in Egypt." June 2, 2017. https://plan-international.org/press-releases/female-genital-mutilation-still-killing-girls-egypt.

Plo, Kouie, Kouadio Asse, Dohagneron Sei, and John Yenan. "Female Genital Mutilation in Infants and Young Girls: Report of Sixty Cases Observed at the General Hospital of Abobo (Abidjan, Cote D'Ivoire, West Africa)." *International Journal of Pediatrics* (2014): 1–5. http://dx.doi:10.1155/2014/837471.

Population Reference Bureau. "Women and Girls at Risk of Female Genital Mutilation/Cutting in the United States." February 5, 2016. https://www.prb.org/us-fgmc/.

Redins, Larisa. "Understanding Cyberterrorism." *Risk Management* 59, no. 8 (October 2012): 32–35. http://libproxy.nps.edu/login?url=https://search.proquest.com/docview/1173888997?accountid=12702.

Rosenthal, Emilio. "Anti-FGM Legislation Is Not an Unconstitutional Measure." *The McGill International Review*, January 14, 2019. https://www.mironline.ca/anti-fgm-legislation-is-not-an-unconstitutional-measure.

Rushwan, Hamid. "Female Genital Mutilation: A Tragedy for Women's Reproductive Health." *African Journal of Urology* 19, no. 3 (September 2013): 130–133. https://doi.org/10.1016/j.afju.2013.03.002.

Schmid, Alex, editor. *The Routledge Handbook of Terrorism Research*. Abingdon, NY: Taylor and Francis, 2011.

Serour, G.I. "Medicalization of Female Genital Mutilation/Cutting." *African Journal of Urology* 19, no. 3 (September 2013): 145–49. https://doi.org/10.1016/j.afju.2013.02.004.

Sesay, Alusine. "Sierra Leone: Government Accused of Being Silent about Combating FGM." *Medium*, February 7, 2017. https://medium.com/@premiernews140/sierra-leone-government-accused-of-being-silent-about-combating-fgm-3188c7b292ec.

Sharif, Khadijah. "Female Genital Mutilation: What Does the New Federal Law Really Mean?" *Forhdam Urban Law Journal* 24, no. 2 (January 1997): 409–881 https://ir.lawnet.fordham.edu/cgi/viewcontent.cgi?referer=https://www.google.com/&httpsredir=1&article=1963&context=ulj.

Shell-Duncan, Bettina. "From Health to Human Rights: Female Genital Cutting and the Politics of Intervention." *American Anthropologist* 110, no. 2 (June 2008): 225–36. https://doi.org/10.1111/j.1548-1433.2008.00028.x.

*The Star*. "How Practices and Meaning of FGM Are Changing Tanzania." April 19, 2018. https://www.the-star.co.ke/news/2018/04/19/how-practices-and-meaning-of-fgm-are-changing-in-tanzania_c1746279.

Sweileh, Waleed. "Bibliometric Analysis of Literature on Female Genital Mutilation: (1930–2015)." *Reproductive Health* 13, no. 1 (October 2016): 1–13. https://doi.org/10.1186/s12978-016-0243-8.

Toubia, Nahid. "Female Circumcision as a Public Health Issue." *The New England Journal of Medicine* 331, no. 11 (September 15, 1994): 712–16. https://www.nejm.org/doi/pdf/10.1056/NEJM199409153311106.

Trueblood, Leigh. "Female Genital Mutilation: A Discussion of International Human Rights Instruments, Cultural Sovereignty and Dominance Theory." *Denver Journal of International Law and Policy* 28, no. 4 (September 22, 2000).

United Nations. "Convention on the Elimination of All forms of Discrimination against Women." Accessed September 16, 2018. http://www.un.org/womenwatch/daw/cedaw/recommendations/recomm.htm.

United Nations Human Rights Office of the High Commissioner. "Convention on the Elimination of All Forms of Discrimination against Women." Accessed August 11, 2018. https://www.ohchr.org/en/professionalinterest/pages/cedaw.aspx.

United Nations International Children's Emergency Fund (UNICEF). "Female Genital Mutilation/Cutting: A Global Concern." 2016. https://www.unicef.org/media/files/FGMC_2016_brochure_final_UNICEF_SPREAD.pdf.

———. *Female Genital Mutilation and Cutting: A Statistical Overview and Exploration of the Dynamics of Change*. New York: UNICEF, 2013. https://www.unicef.org/publications/index_69875.html.

———. *Innocenti Insight: The Dynamics of Social Change towards the Abandonment of Female Genital Mutilation/Cutting in Five African Countries*. Florence, Italy: UNICEF Innocenti Research Center, 2010. https://www.unicef-irc.org/publications/pdf/fgm_insight_eng.pdf.

United Nations Population Fund. "Female Genital Mutilation (FGM) Frequently Asked Questions." Accessed July 9, 2018. https://www.unfpa.org/resources/female-genital-mutilation-fgm-frequently-asked-questions.

———. *Implementation of the International and Regional Human Rights Framework for the Elimination of Female Genital Mutilation*. New York: United Nations Population Fund. https://www.unfpa.org/sites/default/files/pub-pdf/FGMC-humanrights.pdf.

U.S. Department of Justice. "Three Indicted for Female Genital Mutilation." April 26, 2017. https://www.justice.gov/usao-edmi/pr/three-indicted-female-genital-mutilation.

U.S. Department of State. "U.S. Government Fact Sheet on Female Genital Mutilation or Cutting (FGM/C)." Accessed August 11, 2018. https://travel.state.gov/content/travel/en/us-visas/visa-information-resources/fact-sheet-on-female-genital-mutilation-or-cutting.html.

Wambura, Joyce. "Masculinities and Femininities in Female Genital Mutilation Ceremonies in Kuria, Kenya." *Culture, Society and Masculinities* 8, no. 2 (October 1, 2016): 120. https://doi.org/10.3149/CSM.0802.118.

World Health Organization (WHO). *Eliminating Female Genital Mutilation: An Interagency Statement*. Geneva, Switzerland: World Health Organization, 2008. https://www.who.int/reproductivehealth/publications/fgm/9789241596442/en/.

———. "Female Genital Mutilation." January 31, 2018. htttps://www.who.int/news-room/fact-sheets/detail/female-genital-mutilation.

———. *Female Genital Mutilation: An Overview*. Geneva, Switzerland: WHO, 1998. http://apps.who.int/iris/bitstream/10665/42042/1/9241561912_eng.pdf.

———. "Prevalence of Female Genital Cutting among Egyptian Girls." Accessed July 20, 2018. http://www.who.int/bulletin/volumes/86/4/07-042093/en/.

———. "Sexual and Reproductive Health: Female Genital Mutilation (FGM)." Accessed May 23, 2018. http://www.who.int/reproductivehealth/topics/fgm/prevalence/en.

THIS PAGE INTENTIONALLY LEFT BLANK

# INITIAL DISTRIBUTION LIST

1. Defense Technical Information Center
   Ft. Belvoir, Virginia

2. Dudley Knox Library
   Naval Postgraduate School
   Monterey, California

Printed in Great Britain
by Amazon